ACKNOW~~LEDGEMENTS~~

I want to thank my husband, Marc, who made it possible for me to focus, and to write my story. Thank you for your patience, and love throughout all the taxing ups & downs that go along with writing a story that was both delicate, and traumatic for me to share. I love you dearly.

Thank you to my sister, Barbie, who is my best friend and confidant. You have been through it all-right by my side. I love you.

I also wish to acknowledge Jenn Fuller who has helped me edit my book along the way, and for helping to organize an art contest for the cover of this book. Thank you, Jenn, for being an important part of this process. You have continued to be "GOD" with skin on for me, and my family countless times. I love and appreciate you.

Lastly I want to acknowledge Roksanna Keyvan, the artist, for creating, and designing the book cover.

DEDICATIONS

I dedicate this book, above all, to my Abba Father.

I also dedicate this book to my boys, Tyler and Dylan, who have given me the courage, the love and fierce determination to break free from all the chains in my life.

This story is for all the people who have to fight, to suit up and show up for life. This book is dedicated to your journeys.

Thank you to everyone whom I have met along the way on my journey. You have all had a part in shaping who I am.

Lastly, this is for that small child who still resides inside of me. That child who is a survivor, and fighter, and who was filled with innocence, and great assurance that she was never alone. The child who had faith, she would one day be saved and brought to safety. The little child who knows: "You are safe now, You are dearly loved."

BELOVED DAUGHTER
BE LOVED DAUGHTER

Prologue

My name is Betty Jean and it's finally time to tell you my story. It's a story about my life, — the good, the bad, the beautiful, the ugly and everything in between.

I am crying as I put pen to paper because I have a dam of emotions about to break. A floodgate is about to erupt inside of me. A lifetime of trials, tribulations, mountains, valleys and highs and lows that I must share with you because I want to have a voice. I want to let others know that no matter what you have been through, *anything* is possible. Anything at all, —- *if* you keep breathing, *if* you keep hoping, *if* you keep dreaming and *if* you keep believing in someone and in something. In my case it is a God who has been a gentleman to me even when I didn't know he was with me.

In those darkest hours, the ones where I didn't know how to say no or how to ask for help, He was with me. For those times when I came to my own rescue He was there, speaking through my lips, because a five-year-old girl couldn't have figured out how to tell a stranger something so clever without being helped by an Angel or a higher power, in my words, God!

But I will save that for later there is so much to say now.

Now is the time. What time is it? It is now. I am brave enough and strong enough and maybe after fifty-one years even a little wise enough, to articulate and describe my process and journey. Maybe at times when I thought about doing this, I didn't feel my life was valuable, different or stable enough to share. But today I hear my heart screaming to get it all out, —to tell others about my secrets, my fears and my dreams. I feel such a floodgate of emotions that are roaring like a lion to be released —without any reservations and without restraint. It's pure unadulterated abandonment of worrying that you won't like me; that you won't love me; that you will reject me, or that you will leave me, walk away and judge me.

It makes sense. I was bullied my whole childhood by my peers, by the neighborhood kids and by my parents. So, of course, I fear you too may look at me with criticism or unfair judgment. But please, I ask you to stay with me. Please stay with me and hear me out. I finally have the courage and heart to tell you everything. Everything that I have held in for so long, for far too long. Before I leave this earth, I just need to tell you all of it.

One day I will be gone, and I don't want to regret one more thing. Not telling you who I really am would be a regret. I want my children to know. I want my family to know. I want you to know. I understand this is a delicate matter as I want to honor others and yet keep the integrity of my truth. My intention is that I can do both. It is my hope that through me revealing this life journey, it will show that we can overcome anything and everything. Today I am proving it, because I'm still alive. I am here, and I am finally writing my story.

Chapter One

Living in Pennsylvania was like living in any northeastern state. It has four seasons, hard workers, cities nearby as well as countryside. I loved the autumn with the trees and all the dancing colors of red, orange and yellow. I loved picking up the leaves that freshly fell and piling them up only to jump into the pile. It seemed to be a lot of work to only create a disaster that in seconds was destroyed, but apparently it was worth it, because I could do it for hours. Funny how life can be that way. So much work for such a small reward. But that was my life a thousand times over.

My father was a hard worker. How he survived life is beyond me. I need to qualify this, because for years I suffered, always questioning why he did what he did to me. But today I understand. It takes a lifetime to realize that hurting people, hurt people. Wounded people, wound people. Don't get me wrong. I have repeated those phrases since I was twenty-three, but only recently have I really believed it.

I loved my dad, just so you know. I was loyal to a fault at times; but I had such a bond with him that I could allow no one to ever know the truth. And I forgave him

7 x 77. I still do forgive him. In fact, I wish I could have just one more cup of coffee with him. But hopefully he is doing that up there with God. That and watching the Philadelphia Eagles play football with a Philly cheesesteak or hoagie in his strong hands.

I am so happy he gets to rest now. He never got to rest. He was so busy his whole life taking care of everyone else. Now he gets to *just be*.

Please forgive me ahead of time if I become emotional and sappy and even at times analytical and tough on my dad. It may happen. In the end, I promise I loved my father. I'm told by others that I probably loved him more than others would have. I guess I just understand he really didn't know how to do it any other way, or he would have.

I must always keep in the forefront of my mind that he was frustrated, hurting and never had a father figure. But this is my story, and there I go again protecting and shielding my dad. Gosh, I do that so well. Even now, I just don't want you to hate him. I feel sorry for him and I wish I could have seen him happier; freed from his demons.

OK, so here it goes.

I was five when I remember being in my backyard. We were next to the train tracks and our yard backed up to a wooded area. I loved running back there with nature and in the open area. There wasn't a tree I wouldn't try to climb. Trees were always my safe place. Climb a tall tree and you can look down on the world and see everything that is going on and no one could see me. I faded. I was invisible. But most importantly, I was safe.

No one could climb like me. I was fearless, and I never worried about the kids hurting me with their fists, their mean words or their ridiculing laughter. I could sit for hours up there and even pretend that I was OK, —that I was safe and that I was tall, —bigger than the small and mean words of those who taunted me.

This day however, I didn't climb a tree. I strolled, and I enjoyed the solitude and freedom of being all alone, away from the chaos at my home. The fights, the flying knickknacks, the pulling of hair, being choked, and witnessing my mom having to endure this— and me trying to intervene, only to become a part of the scene.

It was confusing and terrifying to watch and to be a part of this scene. I wouldn't wish it on anyone at all. It was a daily occurrence for years, — for my entire childhood. So, when I went out on my own to play in the Woods, I was relieved. Until that is, I wasn't.

At five years old, I saw a man who seemed quite old to me (maybe in his forties). I can still see him now even though I only saw him once in my life.

It's hard to forget him when he was so close to me and, what he did to me was so unforgettable.

He innocently, or so I thought, wanted to play Simon Says. It was my favorite game. Of course, I played with him. He was nice to me. He wanted to play with me. A nice man wanted to play a game, that was a first. He took his shirt off and so did I. Then his pants off and so did I. He put his private part onto my stomach and rubbed it, then up to my vagina. Up and down it brushed up against me. I somehow was able to tell him I liked this game (I was terrified) and that I wanted to play it again tomorrow. I cupped my ear with my hand pretending to hear my mom. I said, "I need to go, my mom is calling for me. I don't want to get into trouble."

He cocked his head and smirked this grin. He seemed amused and intrigued, and with a demented look, he said, "Ok." He let me go.

I ran as fast as I could, relieved that I escaped and found my mother who seemed jolted by what I told her. They checked my privates and all I know is, we moved just a few months later. All these years and I never realized until just last month, but my father's shortcomings, his demons, and his wrongdoings, they saved me in the end.

Because of what I had learned by the age of five, I was smart enough to save my own life with that man wearing a train conductors hat, suspenders, and with a very long beard. Had I done what most five-year old kids would have done, which is scream, or try to run away, he could have very easily put his hand over my mouth, choked me, hit my head to the ground, or raped me and left me for dead. But no, my father and our secrets saved me in the end. By no means am I saying it was OK that my father touched me inappropriately. I'm just saying it prepared me for that man who molested me. Isn't it true so many times that the ugly prepares you for the ugliest? Sometimes even death itself.

Chapter Two

My dad, (here I go again) lost his father at age six.
The family was out for a drive in Chester,
Pennsylvania. His sister in the back seat wasn't even
scratched, thankfully. But his father was instantly
killed when the truck hit them head on. The rain was
the culprit my father explained.

Our rides to the country on Sundays are always
reminders to me that he hated driving next to a big
rig truck in the rain. He was terrified of it. Why
wouldn't he be? It crippled his mother, killed his
much older father, and left him in a coma that lasted
for months. I can't imagine awaking to such a
horror— his mother in a wheel-chair and his dad
nowhere in sight. He was left to recover from a
serious head injury, only to need to be his mother's
new right hand.

 Because of this new scenario, he was put into a boy
only school for kids with absent fathers. I remember
seeing his high school yearbook where he was the
only one with ivory skin and blue eyes. I was in
junior high school when I flipped through the pages
of his book, but I never asked. I just found it

interesting.

But I also knew at that time, his one and only friend was a man nicknamed Couch, because he loved to sit on the couch and eat. He was so nice and funny, and my dad loved him. He looked like all the pictures of his high school mates.

My father grew up in Philly. He taught me how to play run the bases and stickball, and he always picked me for his team when my siblings played baseball or basketball. Of course, he did! I was the oldest of the five of us, and quite athletic compared to them I'd say. (However, I was never picked by my class mates. I was always chosen last, as I was dressed in smelly clothes and my hygiene wasn't very good). I was told he'd wished I was a boy. So, it doesn't shock me that I was a tomboy. (I was also informed that my dad didn't want to be drafted in the Vietnam war, so he and my mom planned my arrival right after they married.)

Surprisingly, I was in a pretty dress most of the times when we visited my Grandparents. I believe my mother's parents had a bit to do with that. They were generous with clothes for their grandchildren, complete with purses and white gloves. We only wore them for special occasions like birthdays and holidays that they hosted for the extended family. It's too bad they didn't care for my father. But in their minds, their beautiful blonde hair, blue eyed "Country Club" daughter, literally married the man from the other side of the tracks. They despised him. He just wasn't good enough for her. Mind you, my mother was indeed gorgeous, but with all due respect, she completed only 9th grade in high school. She couldn't drive and she never did learn. She was not completely well in her mind and struggled with basic responsibilities.

In fact, many years later when I was twenty years old, she had her first of many nervous breakdowns and had to be Baker acted. She was diagnosed for the first time at the age of 39 with a severe mental illness. We always knew that there was something not quite right. She would suddenly run across the room when we were little, (the four of us would be sitting on the sofa) and she would blast her 1960's music and would leap and hop in the air while laughing — only to tear up and cry hysterically just moments later. This could last for hours. My sister and my two brothers and I would just follow her with our eyes as if we were watching a tennis match. It was amusing, but confusing. Why laugh and then cry? Then laugh again. But it was our norm. In between those songs, she would feed us. Sometimes it was just one egg to be split between the four of us.

She would scramble the egg, place it on a plate divided into 4 pieces and say, "We are playing a game, who can eat the slowest?" I don't remember who won. We were starving so it might have been David, the youngest of the four of us, because he was slow - literally and mentally challenged. So, I could see him winning that kind of game. Besides, I probably had to help him eat which I did most times. Even to this day I have a special affection towards him. We spend a lot of time together especially holidays and special events.

In my opinion my mom and dad both checked out when he was born. In fact, his head was flat and is to this day, because he was left in his crib or on the bed so often. I'm sure having four kids in four and a half years was difficult enough for my mother at age twenty-two and my dad at age twenty-three. Then add a child who is visibly different, and in those days, even unacceptable. Look, I need to say this. My mom and dad probably did the very best they could with the little they had going for them —mentally, emotionally, and financially, but the one thing my mom *always* had was a spirituality that probably kept her together and moving forward.

She introduced me to God, and when we went to

church, she would sing her lungs out to the hymns at Sunday services. One of her favorites was Amazing Grace. At home she would sing with us kids: Jesus Loves me and Jesus loves the little Children. I still sing both to myself at times.

Especially the last. *"Jesus loves the little children all the children of the world. Red, brown, yellow Black and white they are precious in His sight. Jesus loves the little children of the world"*.

She got her beautiful voice from her mother who loved to sing and taught herself to play the piano. I loved my Grandmother. She was like a second mom to me. I miss her dearly. She knew all my secrets when I got older. I wish I could have told them to her much sooner than I did. I didn't know any better. She is gone now. But every time I see a pink rose, I think of her. I loved the colors green and purple when I was young. But her influence and love for pink became mine as well as I aged. Anyway, the only time I ever felt safe in those days was when my parents would drop me off at Sunday school. The teachers were so sweet to me. They welcomed me, and they said please come back. They were kind, and they didn't raise their voices. They didn't hit me, pull my ear ,put their hands around my neck to choke me, put a pillow over my face, use a belt on me to choke me or spank me. They never tickled me until I was purple and almost passed out. They didn't tear out my hair or laugh at me, or call me, a brat, stupid, fat, or ugly. They Didn't throw me in a closet for hours or send me down to a cold unfinished basement to take care of my siblings. No, they told me about the man named Jesus who loved me and wanted to live inside my heart. I liked being there. It was one hour out of the 168 hours in the week that I felt safe and happy.

So much so, I recall at age nine leaving Sunday school and going to my great grandmother's house like we always did. One Sunday afternoon when I went, I remember praying to myself, " GOD If you are real please have 'mom mom' call out for David." I made it quite tough on God because no one bothered with David, except my sister Barbie and me. And sure enough, I swear to you, I still get choked up as I write this. She called out for my brother: "David come here."

I can still hear her high-pitched voice. I ran to my mom, "Mom did you just hear 'mom mom' call out to David?"

"Yes," she said.

"Mom," I said, "I just prayed to God to have her call

out to David if He was real, and she just did!"

My mom smiled so big and said, "Of course He is real. You know that, and so are angels!"

Let me tell you my friend, never again did I feel alone. Never again did I question if there is a God or not. At age nine, even though people around me acted like there wasn't one, I knew no matter what they did or didn't do, I had a friend to talk to and boy was I chatty with him. Unfortunately, the very people who should have protected me and loved me, betrayed me again and again.

Chapter 3

My father would tell me to go upstairs with him in that hushed tone of his;

"Come on Betty Jean," and I would follow.

I was about nine years old and I would have followed my dad across the world. For starters, I loved him and, secondly, he was huge, 6 foot 2 and almost 300 pounds. Love and fear will direct you anywhere.

This time it was in our new home— the one we moved to after the railroad man prompted us to take off. My father took off the only article of clothing he had on. Boxers, — he loved those boxers. The only problem was, they always exposed that damn thing that I saw way too much of.

He started to dance like a fool. He swung his hips and that ridiculous part of him I should have never seen would start to swing. I can still hear my mom's footsteps coming up the stairs. I think to myself, "Finally, thank God! I can tell her and even show her what her darn husband is doing right now." I feel her presence at the door, and I point to my dad and jump up like a Jack in the box, eager to make her aware of what was happening.

"Mom, look at dad. He has his pants off and he's dancing."

My heart sank when I took my eyes off my mom and then looked back at my dad. His boxers were back up where they belonged.

"What are you talking about Betty Jean?" my father said curtly.

"Mom he just had them off and he was dancing naked."

"You're such a liar Betty Jean" my father proclaimed.

"Yeah, Betty Jean," my mother chimed in, what are you talking about?"

I froze. My mouth opens wide, but nothing came out, no words, and no air. I looked at my father and back to my mother —another tennis match, —the story of my life. They shake their heads and my dad snickers. I walked down the stairs slowly and I heard nothing. I felt nothing. I went to the nearly empty refrigerator and opened it. I reached for the only three items that were inside, bread, lettuce, and mustard. I made a sandwich —and then another and another. I ate three sandwiches in minutes. It was the first time I would learn to stuff myself—in order to punish myself, to numb myself. Filling myself with food became predictability —a friend that allowed me to keep control of at least one thing. Those three sandwiches kept me from feeling anything. It would be many years later before I would truly feel again.

Chapter 4

I liked our Saturdays and Sundays. We had picnics, and at age ten I ate everything in sight. Ham and cheese sandwiches, potato and macaroni salad and potato chips were favorites. The Wawa lemonade was my mom's and my favorite beverage.

Dad? He loved the iced tea, and he would even out eat me. His drug of choice in life was also food. He stuffed his emotions away like I did. He waited hand and foot on his mother after his father's death. He cooked, cleaned, and even into his adulthood bathed her, and put her on the bed pan. My mom hated that. They fought all the time about it, but it was my father's inability to say no to his mom that kept him obligated to her. Picnics with my family were a reprieve from being privately tortured in our home. In public, we appeared to be such a normal, big happy family.

The exception, of course, was the people we would randomly meet. My dad imposed on them to share their food with us. We always had much less than the others. Look, I know he was just trying to feed his kids. I get it, believe me. The picnics we had always included a few new friends. He would introduce himself to them in the hopes of getting more snacks for all of us.

He wasn't all bad. In fact, he worked like a dog to provide for all of us. My mom couldn't work. She was home with us, and of course, we may have raised her more than she raised us. But at least she was in the house. Dad worked as a prison guard at night, and during the day at a packaging facility. Sometimes he would even work a double shift. With a fifth child on the way, he had to work more than ever.

Anyway, I liked our picnics and long rides on the weekends. It felt a lot less crazy than being indoors with all of us screaming, fighting, and crying. The outdoors brought calmness and a great picture of what would have been nice indoors. We made a great public display of fun, family and unity. Boy, could we act. *(If they only knew the truth.)*

But, how could they? I was so great at going along with the fabricated story. I also believed our act.

"Don't tell anyone Betty Jean. Don't tell your teachers I scratched your eye. Tell them it was the cat."

"Ok mom."

"Don't tell them that your lip is split because I punched you, just say you ran into something" dad says. "If you tell anyone, they will take me away, and I will never see you again. Your brothers and sisters will all be sent away, and we'll be split up and you won't see us again."

I pledged to my parents and to myself, that I would never tell anyone. I loved my daddy and mommy. I loved my siblings. My goodness, we do have the best family ever. They will never take us away. We not only have it OK, we have it great. Look at us, we are one big happy family.

Every single time a teacher or a nurse asked me about my weekly black and blues, scratches, or dark eyes, I had an alibi backed by a big sweet smile. My sister who is only fourteen months younger than I am couldn't live the lie any longer. She advocated for herself as well as the rest of us. She told me that she told the school officials who in turn told social services. When they came to our house, only my sister and mother were there. My mom was both in denial and terrified for her life I'm sure. She was able to perform a stellar production and convince the visitors that all was well in our humble abode, and they left. Poor Barbie asked for help, they came, but no one intervened, and me? I kept the show going out of fear of never seeing her and the rest of my siblings again, like we were the cast of Little House on the Prairie or the cast of the Walton's tv show —- if only we were….'*'Goodnight John Boy, Goodnight Barbara, Goodnight David, Goodnight mommy and daddy, Goodnight cruel world.* "

And then the nightmares would come. I dreamt cave men were running after the cave women and they were naked. I screamed at night. My mom came in next to my bed, and I was crying, and I couldn't sleep. I went to school and I was sad, but I kept smiling. I was tired because I couldn't sleep at night from the nightmares. I went into the bathroom at night and took a quick bath to wash away the night sweats and my father watched me at the door. I had no privacy. My parents were called into the school when I was in kindergarten. Why? Because of the behavior I did. Under the chairs I could cross my legs, and it felt so good to rub them together. I could do this in every single class, and no one would know or, so I thought. I'd enjoy those moments all day until I was spent. This was the only good feeling I can remember. The other moments I looked out the window of my classroom and stared. I didn't really hear too much of what the teacher said. The odd time I did was because I was being a smart Alec and making fun of the teacher. I would be moved to the front of the class next to the teacher's desk. I would pay attention then. I didn't like it because I had to be attentive, present, and it didn't feel nearly as good as my own little world. It didn't much matter. I wasn't liked by the teachers or by the kids and now, by my dad. Once I disclosed his dumb dance to mom, he couldn't look at me unless it was with disgust. The only place that felt somewhat protected was when I was reading a book or with my headphones on and my music blaring. And of course, in God's house, Church. Everything and everyone else were a farce. I didn't know that then I was just going through the motions one day at a time, waiting for the day I could leave this crazy and deranged place.

"Hey dad," I asked when I was about ten years old in our station wagon on our way home from the local grocery store: "How old do you have to be to leave home?"

"Seventeen. Why?"

"Dad I will be leaving when I turn seventeen. "

"You know Betty Jean, you are not like the rest of us and you never were."

That stung, that penetrated. I used to think it was so bad. I took those words and allowed them to seep deep into my bones. I felt different. I was different. I kept people away by my words, and by my actions. My "come to me, but don't get too close to me" behavior.

Today I realize I am different, but *not* because I am so bad, but because I am hyper sensitive to others, and at times too on guard and distrusting of others. I had to be hyper-vigilant in discerning what mood and state of mind my parents were in so I could be prepared for what course of action was next. Do I run or remain quiet in hopes that they will be calmed? So maybe my dad was correct, I wasn't like him but If I was anything else, I believed I'd be out of my mind. No one saved us when Barbie raised the red flag. No one questioned my cameo performances. No one came to our rescue. That is why I am so grateful that last month I finally realized that my dad's sick demons helped me in the end. My survival techniques helped to rescue me at five years old, and later, at the age of nineteen. I can't believe I have allowed so many wrong people into my life.

I didn't trust, but if they felt familiar, I would let them in. I let the wrong ones in every single time without even realizing it until it was too late. I wish I could have done more than just save me each time. I wish I could have avoided the unhealthy people that I had to save myself from. But no, they had smooth tongues, and I had a broken way of choosing. I looked for those who looked different, but in the end they were all the same. My goodness, how many times does it takes to get it

right?   In my case, it was four.   But first, let's back up
to a time before any of them.

Chapter 5

Food was my automatic first choice for comfort and easement.   But suddenly, it wasn't working for me anymore.   In fact, it was working against me now.

I didn't like the reflection I was seeing in the mirror. I was always trying to go on a calorie reducing diet. I hated running back then or doing any serious exercise. I was much too top heavy, and it was terribly uncomfortable to run.   (Go figure, because many years later I would fall in love with the sport of running.   Of course, I had about 30 pounds less to carry around by then). My pants were snug, and my belly was extended from all the binging and the pin worms I had contracted from our German Shepherd and running outside without shoes. I lived with them for many years. It wasn't until I discovered laxatives at age 17 that I finally was free of those butt scratching critters. It breaks my heart that I had to be so uncomfortable for years when a simple, inexpensive medicine would have destroyed those tiny white worms. I don't know if it was because of lack of money or lack of education on my parents' part. Either way 12 years of it was maddening and embarrassing. My mom would lay me on her lap face down and try to pick them out, one by one to no avail.

I had no self-control back then. But nothing seemed able to fill the "parent sized hole" and the "God sized hole". I would start to fill those "holes" with not only food, but now with alcohol and pot.

My father and mother decided to move us to South Florida—- to my mom's parents— the very family that they fought about relentlessly. My father had been laid off from work and we needed some help; so, we moved in with my grandparents who had just moved to Florida full time after years of being snowbirds.

I liked it there. We got to swim in a real outdoor pool in this massive yard and there was delicious homemade food. There was enough for all of us and the violence stopped. At my new school, I could reinvent myself. No one knew how I had been bullied back in Pennsylvania. Not that I had many friends now, but at least I didn't have any enemies either.

The kids were racier here. A boy came up to me and asked me if I was still a virgin and if I smoked pot. I replied no to both questions. I came home and asked my uncle (who was still living at home with my grandparents), "What is a virgin"? He looked at me and said, "You need to ask your parents that question."

Uncle Frank was one of the few men in my life that I loved being around. He was funny, kind and always there for us when we were growing up and when we all lived in Pennsylvania. In fact, he was part of the opposing team for our family baseball and basketball gatherings. He seemed to really like me, and my dad. In my opinion, he must have mediated and buffered the conversations his parents and mine had. He could be neutral, and objective. Thank God for such a nice, level-headed uncle.

Anyway, I was indeed a virgin my parents said. And so, I was, for longer than most of my peers. We only stayed in South Florida for a few months. The fighting was too much for my parents and my grandparents, so off we went again back to Pennsylvania. I was disappointed because I liked being in Florida with my extended family. I was safe, clean and relaxed there. We stayed in South Philadelphia with my parents' friends for a few months. We slept on a floor where rats would crawl on us. They were kind to help us, but I couldn't wait to leave. We settled outside of Lancaster, a college town in Millersville, PA. We moved into a three-bedroom, one-bathroom apartment complex. There were seven of us now. I didn't love sharing a room with my 2 sisters, but I loved that Lisa, the youngest, was out of her crib now because I could take her for long walks to get us ice cream. I adored her like she was my own. It was better here than anywhere else I had lived. Why? Because, once again, I had a fresh start and for the first time, I made some friends. My best true friend was Elizabeth. She was awesome. I would go to her place which was a hotel her family managed. I got to sleep over often.

We would go bicycle riding, play PAC MAN and hang out at the local mall together. I felt so happy to be cool and included. You don't realize how much you miss something that you never had, until you finally get it. I was truly grateful to have her and some other friends in my life. The other girls and boys I met were a year older than me. I was all of 11 years old and they were 12. Some were even 13!

One Friday at the neighborhood pool, we devised a plan to buy alcohol from a local pizzeria. I asked a young college student if he would please buy me a bottle of beer and I would buy him one in return. All my babysitting jobs and cleaning college boy's bathroom toilets for a dollar in the neighborhood had paid off. I had my own stash of money now. The college kids always came through and even complemented me for being such a good business woman and negotiator at such a young age. I learned to be whatever I needed to be in life. This was easy.

I would go to the Woods afterwards to drink with one of my new-found friends. When I drank the first sips, I wasn't too impressed by the taste, but boy did the warmth going down my throat and into my veins feel comforting. No wonder the song *Comfortably Numb* by Pink Floyd became my new favorite song.

I got a small buzz. I laughed. I got silly. I didn't care what I said. ..... I felt accepted by the others. When I walked out of the Woods that day, I said goodbye to little Betty Jean and hello to the new, carefree, free spirit preteen. I no longer sat alone in the bedroom, locked in a closet with Barbie because we were put there for hours, or a damp basement where I was imprisoned by my secrets. We are as sick as our secrets. I didn't know it then and it would take another 12 years to figure that out. But for then, at the age of 11, I got a taste of freedom, solace and relief —even if it was just for a couple of hours.

Chapter 6

I climbed through the window and as I dropped to the floor, my mother grabbed me by my hair and started pushing me. For the first time in my life, I pushed her back. I was used to being beaten by my parents and then apologized to with endless tears streaming from their eyes.

But this time it was different. My mom was justified in her anger. I was drunk and high and caught red handed. So much for the pillows on my bed being dressed up with the shirt, pants and sneakers. It had looked realistic before leaving the apartment, but now it just looked pathetic. She found me out ...It was great while it lasted those last few months, but now I was grounded. No more sneaking out for hours doing acid, pot and amaretto shots. For my punishment, I had to go to a Bible study with my sister Barbie, who like me, was also getting into her own trouble……. They found her a few days later. She had just been picked up from running away.

 Now we were both in a car with a friend of my mom's driving us to a place for troubled teens. It was in the city of Lancaster and we had no idea what to expect. When we got there, it wasn't anything we were anticipating...

I had a Roach clip feather placed in my hair. I was wearing jeans and shit kickers. We were as high as a kite.

There were about twenty teens there and we stuck out like a sore thumb. We were the only two white kids in the room. No one seemed to care.... They sang some songs and a lady spoke about God and how he forgives us. She asked if anyone wanted to give their heart to Jesus?

I don't know why it was so easy for me. Maybe the memories of being in Sunday school came back. But that feeling of being welcomed, wanted, and cared for was instantaneous and that night I raised my hand and said, " Yes, I do. I want to give my heart to Jesus."

I knew there was a God. I had not forgotten the encounter I'd had with my 'mom mom ' at age nine, but this was the first time I had sincerely and publicly said it out loud to Him and others.

After the Bible study, my sister jumped up and ran over to a very tall man and started talking animatedly. She was visibly upset, and she was crying. I ran over ready to protect her. (It wasn't like her to be so emotional.) I thought that they were fighting. But instead, to my dismay, she announced to me with great emotion, "Betty Jean, this man was at my school when I ran away. He saw that I wasn't OK and asked me if I was all right. He said he would pray for me."

The man hadn't known that she had just run away, but he noticed that she seemed distraught. And here we were a couple of days later in a home where everyone was praying, singing and loving each other!

She hugged him and he smiled. This man, a police office, had prayed for my sister and here we were in the same Bible study! Talk about an answered prayer.

I gave up my drinking and smoking and even threw out all my heavy rock albums (but not my Pink Floyd). I exchanged it for an Amy Grant, Twila Paris, Sandy Patty, Michael W. Smith and the Imperials cassette tapes. I began reading the Bible instead of the horror paperbacks and began volunteering at the teen center. We had good wholesome and clean fun.

My favorite part of this new community was the weekend and summer camp. I went one time as a camper and the next two years as a camp counselor. What fun I had and what a great change took place in me. I started to do better in my high school classes. My relationships changed and I included my new friends in my home life. I was more understanding and more "present." I was having the best time with my new family and friends……. If only it could have lasted ….But as my dad would often say , " It's better than a sharp stick in the eye."

Chapter 7

At camp, I met so many teenagers like myself from the inner cities of Philadelphia, Washington DC and Lancaster. I learned to play Double Dutch jump rope with Shortcake and Letty, two of my friends. (We reunited just 2 years ago) We would sing gospel songs, invent skits and perform them at night and ride horses and hike in the day together. I love how much fun I had with them. We laughed and had the time of our life together.

I started to like boys— some of whom had Jeri curls. Many of my new friends had similar backgrounds to me and we all loved God. I believe God took me out of my hell of self-destruction and my crazy house and brought me home to this suitably named haven for teens. I also started to attend morning Bible study in my high school.

Pastor J, who led our group, also attended a local church in Lancaster. I attended both the high school Bible study and the one at the church. He taught me how much Jesus loved me and how He had a special place for the people of Israel. I knew nothing about the Jewish people then, but I loved his huge heart for us teens. He was so humble, and he was always laughing. The laughter came from deep down,— not manic or pretend and not drug induced. Like my uncle, he was another safe man in my life. He was like a big brother or like a second dad. Being part of his youth group and the Haven for teens group continued to keep me very busy and far away from my house.

I may not have had the healthiest of parents, but I was provided people along the way that filled in and taught me love and, without even realizing it, some parenting and family structure. At seventeen, as I promised, I finished high school and was ready to leave my home.

I had a few jobs along the way— sales and telemarketing, babysitting, shoveling snow, and a nurse's aide position in a nursing home facility where I worked the graveyard shift in the summer. By now I had talked to Pastor J about going into more ministry and decided on becoming a missionary for a conservative denomination. I'd hoped I could go to some far off place like Costa Rica or Puerto Rico, but all they had available was upstate New York. I was a bit disappointed, to say the least, but I was eager and willing to go anywhere to volunteer and serve for this organization that had been so kind to me. I was also getting "the heck out of Dodge " —as I voiced that day in our station wagon.

My scores were too low to go into the army. I couldn't concentrate in school to learn and I was also considered too overweight. I tried to lose weight and was able to get to the required number. But I had no resources or help with getting my SAT scores up. I wanted to be a soldier for our country. In some ways I feel I have been. I can certainly relate to how some of them feel after going through my own combat. Anyway, I was told instead to go serve and be a missionary in the community of Corning, NY. I was leaving! Wahoo!

A few days before I packed and left, my dad said to me by our community pool: "Betty Jean you don't have to leave. You can stay here and continue to work as a nurse's aide. I won't charge you to stay here. Please stay with us."

"Dad I already signed up and I'm leaving,— but I am still your little girl," I said sweetly but with confidence.

He responded, "Once you're gone, you can't come back. You will never be the same."

"I know that dad." And to myself I said: " *I'm banking on that* ," and I turned and walked away without looking back.

The house in upstate New York was quite big and the other volunteers serving were quite nice. I was by far the youngest at age seventeen and, in fact, they had never had a volunteer as young as me. But because I would turn eighteen in a couple of months, and my resume was quite full of leadership positions, i.e. (camp counselor, self-lead Vacation Bible school for the neighborhood kids, nurse's aide and being the eldest of five kids) they accepted me.

 At first I'm sure they were quite pleased and even at times impressed, but that would quickly change. When you grow up in a home that is led by chaos, an undiagnosed mentally challenged mother and a raging father, and then you are placed in a healthy, calm and structured house, all hell breaks loose. I honestly thought this was a strange place... My goodness was it mundane. I was in such denial of my life. *Denial:* Don't Even Know that I am Lying or *Denial*: Don't even! No! I Am lying!

I thought this place was bizarre and it obviously wasn't them,— but you couldn't have convinced me of that back then. I was like an ostrich sticking my head in the sand. "Nothing is happening here. Isn't life splendid?". I was ignoring the obvious, but I wasn't ready to come up for air. So, I did what any normal ostrich does, I kept my head buried in a hole with just enough air to barley breathe.

November 12th, 1984, my sister Barbie came to visit me in New York. She came with such horrible news that I took responsibility for. She was no longer interested in living for God. My parents were doing badly and so were all the neighborhood kids that I had taught during my self-led vacation Bible school.

I blamed myself. If I would have stayed in Pennsylvania, Barbie would still be God fearing, my

39

parents would be happy and saved! If I had not left the community of teenagers that I loved, they would still be on fire for the Lord. — As if I had that much power. I also missed my siblings, especially Barbie and my baby sister Lisa.

I think if I were to have died back then, I would have seen someone else's life flash before my eyes instead of my own. I was so enmeshed with saving others that I didn't realize that I was drowning and needed the life preserver even more than anyone else! Bless my heart. In no way am I saying that I shouldn't have loved and helped others. That was an altruistic and unselfish trait. I just didn't realize that you can't give away what you don't really possess yourself.

I did something that day that both saddens and puzzles me. Yes, of course, a psychology text book would back up my choice. But really, me? Try to take my own life?

When Barbie and I finished our talk about how badly everyone and everything was back home, I bought a bottle of rum at the liquor store. I drank it all with her —and as many people will do after getting drunk— we exchanged some harsh words. But the ones I heard her say that pierced my soul was that I was a hypocrite and not really a Christian. It stung me....

I don't know why, but when she left to go to the local YMCA to play volleyball with another volunteer peer, I stayed back in the house alone. I proceeded to take the bottle of back pain pills that were prescribed to me just days before for my lower back issues that I believe were from being thirty pounds overweight. As soon as I took them, I knew it wouldn't be enough to do the job, so I ran across the street to a local drug store and bought sleeping pills. I put all of them into my mouth. I walked back into the house and as I started to become disoriented, I took a magic marker to the wall and wrote: *'I love you dad, mom, Barb, John, David and Lisa and I am sorry.'*

I was starting to lose consciousness and I became terrified. I picked up what felt like a 20-pound phone receiver and dialed the local YMCA . I told her it was an emergency and to please page my sister Barbara. I panicked and I admitted to the woman on the receiving line "I just tried to kill myself." I clutched my Bible that was next to the phone and I held it. I was awake for a few more seconds and then the next thing I saw was my sister and fellow missionaries with tears rolling down their cheeks looking down at me and hysterically crying. I noticed a paramedic and then —blackness.

I was just seventeen years old and it was November 12th, my mother's 37th birthday. Was I making a statement? Perhaps, I don't know. That is just a fact. But deep down, I believe I didn't want to die.   I just didn't want to live either — at least not like I had been. I must have been screaming for help for something —

41

and yet it wasn't the time for me yet —and wouldn't be for many more years.

I awoke to the sounds of beeping. Over my head was a monitor. I was exhausted and there were tubes up my nose, down my throat and in my arm. I felt blood between my legs and when I picked up my gown, I discovered a tube(which they called a catheter) inside my vagina. I couldn't move without pain from all the apparatuses. I felt stuck, a prisoner in this bed — but that wasn't new to me. I had been a hostage and prisoner all my life— to my secrets, my demons— and to my dad. I still loved him. I had a bond to him —a trauma bond— but a bond just the same. Not being able to tell anyone the truth is exhausting, but having to perform like everything is fabulous is just unfair. I was so tired of pretending, but I didn't realize it then. No— the show must go on! My life and my family's lives depended on it. What a terrible burden to put on a child. But I took the job and as far as anyone knew, I was still a stellar employee— until now.

I called out , "Hello?"

" Hello," a nurse replied. " Good, you're awake. Hey, listen we had to pump your stomach twice . We almost lost you twice— once from the overdose and the second time when we discovered you are allergic to penicillin. Make sure you never use penicillin in the future or you can die. "

"OK," I whispered, and fell back asleep.

When I awoke again, it was the next day and the NY pastor from the Church I attended was praying outside of my hospital curtain; "God please forgive her for trying to commit suicide and for trying to take her life. Please help her."

I started to chime in with him and say my own prayer: "Yes! God whoever is beside me in the next bed please help her and thank you for saving her." The pastor opened the curtain and looked down at me with a dumb founded but compassionate look and says: "Betty Jean, no one else is in here. I am praying for you!"

For the first time, a light bulb went off inside of me. I thought we were praying for someone else. That was the story of my life. I always tried to help everyone else. But maybe, just maybe, it was too painful and overwhelming for the "help" to be for me at that time. I was so out of touch with reality and the truth I wouldn't have known.

I just know that when they released me and took me to a counselor, I smiled hugely and answered every question with: "My family is wonderful. I am happy. I just did this because I was drunk,"…. and they believed me. I believed me.

Instead of seeing me again, they told the house leader that I was fine. I needed to just not drink again. My stellar performance was so believable that I even believed it!

It's too bad we didn't have the resources to put me into a Playhouse theater program because I would have thrived. Little did I know that this was the beginning of the end for me. I pulled my bridges up and decided that God wasn't ready for me yet, so I would live 100% for him on earth again. I would exercise daily and eat healthy and get back to displaying the warrior.

I lost a few pounds and I fell in love for the first time with my fellow missionary. He volunteered at a local mental hospital as part of his church service. I visited the elderly in a local nursing home as part of my service. I sang songs with the senior citizens; we prayed. I read the Bible to them and took them out on walks while I pushed them in their wheelchairs . I smiled while I listened to them for hours on end, but they never knew the pain or the sadness I carried deep down. I couldn't fault them for that. It was me that was the master at pretending. If you're not able to tell yourself the truth you cant tell anyone else either.

My new boyfriend and I were the youth group leaders in the community. We organized bowling trips, Bible studies and ice cream outings. We were quite the pair! I believed my dad would have been proud —even if he never said anything…. He had to be because my boyfriend was like all of his high school classmates.

My new boyfriend was kind to me. We prayed and read the Bible together. We laughed and we kept a secret…… We could not let anyone know about our relationship because that was one of the rules — don't get involved with the opposite sex! So we honored each other and stayed away from any sexual encounters. But we certainly broke the rule of no relationships and so once again I was back in my element of keeping a secret.

It was fun and, in my view, harmless — until we were discovered kissing in my room. That was the end of our secret! We had to break up or he had to go... and so he left and went back to the Bronx in New York.

I was devastated. He was my friend, my companion, and my first boyfriend . It didn't matter that it had only been four months . I fell hard— because after I had tried to kill myself , he had been there for me — emotionally, physically and spiritually.

I wrote him letters. I prayed and I cried. I missed him. But I continued to work out and lose weight and even thrived with my responsibilities. And then one day, he was back in the community. Not as a fellow volunteer, but just a regular guy living down the street . We were back in love and together again! He would workout with me at the YMCA and encouraged me. We were inseparable after my commitment to my daily responsibilities. So much so, that eventually we had our first sexual encounter. We were so awkward — neither of us knowing what the heck we were doing— but the blood revealed that we were successful in becoming one. It was our first time together and also the last.

He wasn't too pleased about me not being "more into it," but I was scared and inexperienced with going "all the way". How could I be any other way?

For the first time, he was a bit disappointed in me and I felt like I had let him down. The community didn't look fondly on us either ... Only *we* seemed to accept *us*. The chirping from our community being opposed to us as a couple began to take its toll. We were the only interracial couple in our area and I couldn't understand why we weren't accepted and celebrated, — but we weren't ….

I had lost all my weight and boys started to really notice me. Girls started to notice him. We both agreed to take a break and eventually, we broke up. I went from being a prude —an innocent girl— to becoming a woman on a mission. I wanted to be loved, adored and worshipped. How on earth does an "ugly, fat, stupid " kid like me, become pretty, desirable and sharp? Let me count the ways….

Chapter 8

I began to meet gorgeous college guys and I was having the time of my life at the local Community College. I ended up being asked to leave a month early from my one year commitment to the ministry because I was seen with a guy at a car show outside of church. I had a beer in my hand. One of the teens from the youth group saw me and notified the headquarters .

"We are sorry to tell you, but you must go now. You are becoming a liability to us."

'Don't you know who I am?' I thought. I didn't say it, but I thought it. I had volunteered eleven months of my life and you were telling me to leave? **I was incensed! How could they?** But they had a reputation to keep and I wasn't a poster girl for conservatism. In reality, they could have asked me to go earlier that year, in November, after my overdose. But I had taken the challenge personally to heart. *I'll show them!*

Thankfully, the month before, I had assisted one of the senior citizens who needed my help to take him outside for his daily cigarette. Unbeknownst to me, he was very wealthy and had no kids. His wife had died and because of my daily walks and talks with him , he asked me what I was going to do after I left the ministry. I told him. " I don't know," — and I didn't.

" Can you go to college?" he asked.

"No, I have no money," I said matter of factly.

"Well, what about your family?" he asked.

"Oh no! I don't want to go back there."

"Well, if you could go to college , what would you study, nursing?"

"Oh no! I hate blood. I would be a counselor to help people." (Of course I would. Let's keep trying to fix and rescue the world.)

"OK!" he said. "Sign up at the Community College tomorrow and ask for the lady in admissions. She will take care of you!"

"Really?!" I said with surprise!

"Yes!" he answered quickly.

"Oh, thank you so much! "

I didn't believe it until I got there and sat down with the nice admissions woman. But yes, I was signed up as a student! I left with the schedule for Human Services, Psychology, Counseling 101, English and Math! I was beyond grateful and blown away. I went from uneducated and unlearned to a college kid! At that time, I was the only one in my family to attend college. But instead of taking it seriously, I drank every evening when I didn't have a test or project due. How I got A's and B's was a miracle, and a lot of coffee for sure!

I studied very hard, and for my reward, I would attend a couple of lady's nights in the college bars.... With my new figure and long pretty hair, I met the cutest boys who doted over me.   Well, did that feel good! I was finally getting some attention!

I bought new fashionable clothes. I traded in my long dresses for fitted jeans. I wore fitted shirts. I went from being unnoticed to being popular.   I went from being bullied, ridiculed and overlooked, — to being flattered and accepted. One day in class one of my schoolmates told me a bunch of friends from class were going out for wings and a drink in a local restaurant would I like to come along. I was delighted to be included. He picked me up from my residence and when we arrived there was only one boy. The others he explained were not able to come as they had to study for tests. We each had two drinks and he told me he would take me home, but could we please stop at his place to take his dog out quickly to pee. Of course, I said yes. I didn't want his dog to be uncomfortable. It was only a few minutes more. When we arrived, he ran in and asked me to come in and see his puppy. I dashed in and when he closed the door, he locked it and put his hand over my mouth from behind and did things to me I just recently have been able to talk about and process. Being sodomized and having someone do such an unthinkable act without permission and trying to break free and escape is painful on so many levels. Afraid for my life as I was only 125 pounds and no match for his much larger frame. He was a strong athlete I whimpered and hoped it would stop much sooner than later. He made it clear if I said anything, he would ruin my reputation and deny it. I was stunned, mortified and embarrassed. The shame stayed with me and I avoided him like the plague. I never told anyone. I buried it but I believe it was very much alive in me without realizing it. In fact, I wrote this book and after many revisions added it here rather than just near the end as it was so traumatic for me. But I am choosing to dismiss worrying about "saving face" and instead saving my soul, saving myself and maybe even you or someone you may know. I am as sick as my secrets. Even the ones I hide from me.

By now upstate New York was not the same for me I gained about 20 pounds in a matter of a few months from the endless binging on food and beer after that horrific night , so when I visited my rich grandmother in South Florida during spring break , I knew that I had to come back to where I always wanted to be— so I transferred to school in Florida.

I flew down to begin my new life — another reinvention. But this was very different from the first time. This was a complete makeover. I went from wholesome to being risqué in a matter of months; from being chubby and pretty to being wild and carefree. I lived for the limelight in the clubs, the loud music, the opulence of the chandeliers, the brand name suits, fancy dresses and fancy cars and the older men with yachts and mansions. There were endless ladies' nights with free alcohol, hors d'oeuvres and dancing. This was my dream come true!

I was rocketed into another dimension. I went from my hands in the air worshipping Jesus to men holding dollar bills up to me and worshiping me! I didn't even realize that I was such a decent dancer, but put on Prince, Whitney Houston or Guns and Roses, put alcohol in me, and I could go all night long. The eyes of the crowd on me was titillating. I remember that familiar look, — eyes undressing me, —cooing, whistling and cat calling.

Back when I was a child in the drive-in movie theater, my entire family would watch the G rated movie, Bambi, then a second movie which was PG, and then lastly, an x-rated Tom and Jerry cartoon would be shown. The only two awake would be my father and me. My mom had asked him earlier to leave after the second movie, but he chose not to. —No wonder I needed to self-stimulate all the time as a little girl; well that and being touched.

 Now I was making my own sensual show. It lasted only a few months, but I had never made money so quickly *and* it felt good to be noticed! Besides, performing was my forte and it was fun, — until it wasn't.

My new boyfriend wasn't too pleased about me dancing. When he found out, he demanded that I quit. He was very protective and jealous, and he was disgusted that I would dance with no shirt on and allow others to see my young body. So, I opted to work as a hostess in a restaurant. I made peanuts by comparison, but because we lived together, he assured me he would take care of all the bills.

One day he came home and saw my girlfriend and me in our bikinis, riding our beach cruiser back from Fort Lauderdale Beach. We were drunk out of our minds. He took me inside the house, grabbed my long hoop earrings, and started to shake my head back and forth like my mom and dad used to do.

I froze. I stayed calm as he tore the earring from my ear — splitting my ear in the process. It bled everywhere…. He pushed me, but I continued to remain calm. I did what I had learned to do 1000 times as a child. I play acted…. I played dead, like an injured animal. This was old hat for me. I was terrified, but instinctively I knew what I had to do. When he tired and collapsed, he started to cry and apologize —just as my father had done many years ago. I smiled softly and told him it was OK… I reassured him that I was fine. He fell asleep as I lay there all night, waiting for the sun to rise. When he kissed me goodbye before he went to work, I waved to him like nothing ever happened. But, when I saw him pull away, I packed as quickly as I could. I jumped into my first car (I had just bought a month prior) and went to the police. I got a restraining order against him.

I was tormented all my life. I had left home at seventeen and there was no way another man was going to pick up where my dad had left off.

He found me days later, hiding at my Uncle's apartment. He tore my car apart. We called the police and they found him immediately. He was arrested, and he was encouraged to move away. However, it was not the last time the wrong hands would touch my heart and soul.

After he moved away, I went back to dancing for a few more months and modeled lingerie in local bars in the afternoon.

Looking back, it was ridiculous... but so were most of the things I did. In the moment it made sense. I made good money and I was able to party and have fun. It seemed glamorous to me, compared to my wholesome and conservative life before Florida. But truth be told, I had lost my morals, my values and my belief system. I was living a double life. I *said* I loved God, but I didn't show it with this new lifestyle. When you want to know what someone believes, watch what they do. My God became alcohol, men, attention and food.

One day after a shift of heels, lingerie and endless dancing, the manager and owner of the establishment took me home where we smoked something that I thought was a joint. But when I came to, he was standing over me mortified and there were two paramedics asking if I was ok.

I responded, What are we doing? Now they looked mortified. After a series of questions, they suggested I go to the local hospital saying I had just had a grand mal seizure. I said, "OK." But instead I went back to the club.

I sat and watched everyone make money and for the first time, I felt darkness like I had never felt before. It's hard to feel when you are a moving target. But sitting there that night, I felt dirty. However, I'd have to do a few more things that week that I can't even repeat. After that week, I quit. I quit that life, that disgusting evil and wicked life.

I went back to working as a waitress. When I went out one evening for a few drinks after my shift, I met a man who told me he had just moved to the area. He bought me a drink. We talked and I got drunk. He took me home and as I had expected and accepted by now, we would be having some crazy sex. However, when he took me into a second bedroom, he reached into a closet with a few smocks, — a big long dress like my grandma would wear. He said, "This is my Aunts. Put it on and get some sleep. There is a bed for you, and I will be in the other room."

What? Shocked, I chuckled thinking he was going to say, 'just kidding,' but he wasn't. No man had been so kind to me in Florida. He wasn't going to use me.

I fell asleep and when I woke up in the morning, I saw him looking down at me with compassion. We got coffee and he told me all about himself. He wanted to be a priest, but after meeting me he wasn't so sure. A week later, when we made love for his first time, he decided that he was certain that he wanted to be with me forever.

I loved him. He was kind and he was a hard-blue collar worker. When he would come home from work, we would eat dinner together. I enjoyed him, but as time passed, I found our life too routine and boring. I drank a lot and would get so drunk that I would call him names. "You're so boring. I don't even know what I'm doing with you."

Eventually, he tired of me. He would open the door when I knocked to come into our home, and he would check my breath. Gum never hid the stench.

One night when I went out without him, I met a cute guy who drove me home. We kissed for a long time in his car in front of our house. When I walked into the house, my new fiancé was beside himself.

"I saw you kissing him."

I denied it.

I was great at denying the obvious, but this was it! He was sick of me and so was I. I knew he wanted to end it and so I broke up with him before he could, and I decided to go back to a self help group.

Just a year prior, I had gotten into a car accident. I hit a pole and went through my windshield and was jailed that night. I was court ordered into a fellowship. I went for the time they made mandatory, but I didn't *really* think I was an alcoholic, even though my grandfather had once told me that I was. He had caught me climbing into the house after midnight a couple of times drunk when I lived with my grandparents.

Everyone was old, and I was only twenty. Still, the people were so nice and welcoming, and they said things like "Keep coming back. We will love you until you love yourself."

Well, that was great for all of them I thought, but I just did my ten one-hour sessions that week and left. Now I was back and this time, it was my choice. I needed help. I didn't get into trouble every time I was drinking, but whenever I got into trouble, I had been drinking.

I was sick and tired of being 'sick and tired.' I was running 100 miles an hour and getting nowhere fast. I had finally crashed and burned. I raised the white flag and surrendered. The most important words in my vocabulary, then and even now, are: 'I need help. — Please help me. —I don't know— and thank you. '

It's one thing to know you have a problem, but it's a whole other thing to accept it. It was difficult accepting that I needed help because I was always so busy pretending that I was invincible, strong, and in control. It shattered me to realize that I really wasn't any of those things after all.

I started working at a girls' treatment center where most of them were just a few years younger than me. Most had come from homes like mine, but I thought I could help fix them. It's amazing how I could look at them and know just what to say.

Meanwhile, I was stuffing myself with food, occasional drinks, and lies. But I really wanted to help them. After a few months, I was asked to leave because my behavior, attitude and personality was no different then theirs. I could have been housed there myself.

In the Church hall I went to after I was let go, a woman rose her hand to speak. She was so articulate, smart and funny. I thought I might go up and speak to her afterwards. To my chagrin, she came over to me and said I would like to be your temporary mentor. She handed me her card with her phone number and said to call her every day at 5 PM.

"Call me and we will start some writing as homework together. "

I asked her a few questions, as if I was interviewing her for a job. I wasn't going to have just any mentor I had decided that morning. I would need someone who loved God, went to church and was positive. I discovered she was seeing the same addiction therapist that I was seeing in my new church.

She replied yes to all my questions with laughter. We agreed on our new relationship and she walked away chuckling while I was dead serious.

Looking back, I realize I was a real piece of work. I should have been humbler and more gracious, but the gall of me to have a checklist for a woman who would end up being part of my life changing years was amazing. She was the first woman in many years that I would trust.

"Men will pat your butt" she said, "but a woman will save it!"

She was right and save it she did!

"Write the pros and cons of your drinking." she said.

I did. I did everything she requested, including staying away from the opposite sex for a year.

What? Really?

I did it, but it wasn't easy. So instead of having a boyfriend, I fell in love with Denny's Pecan pie and frozen yogurt from any store. I blew up like Humpty Dumpty. The only problem was, I didn't fall, — in my opinion, I was pushed. And it would take a lot of assistance to put me back together again.

The pros of drinking? I could dance better, and I could make love better! The cons? It was an endless list. Seeing it with my own two eyes was astounding and eye opening. Why the heck would I want to drink when the bad outweighed the good by so much and the bad was so blatant! Blackouts, grand mal seizures, sex with strangers, working in dark places and most and foremost —a disconnection with God.

It was hard to think about God when I was acting like the devil. I missed God and I know he missed me. God never left me. I left him. Seeing my list of pros and cons on that day made me realize it wasn't worth giving up my life to the demons. That list opened my eyes. I wanted to continue as soon as possible with my writing.

"How is God bringing back your soundness of mind?" she asked.

"Soundness of mind? Are you saying I'm insane? "

I was horrified. I was terrified of that being a possibility! My own mother had finally been diagnosed with a couple of mental disorders and chemical imbalances. I feared this would be my future. I wanted nothing to do with being unpredictable, random and erratic! The question riveted me back then. (Of course, once she was medicated properly, she was able to function and was less moody and more well balanced.)

After I calmed down, she explained, "Look, insanity is just doing something over and over again and expecting different results."

Oh, well I knew I was drinking and thinking I'd only have one or two. But I would end up having eight, nine or ten drinks and not know if I would be preaching God to you or climbing up on a table and dancing for you.

I guess I could admit that wasn't the result I was going for. I wanted to drink like a lady and have a glass of wine, but that *never* happened, not once.

OK... So, the fact that I was changing my friends and the places I hung out and that I was hanging out with her and going to counseling was proof God was restoring me to sanity. I was on my way, even if it was just inches. Time, it takes time. It was a process and I had to trust it like I had to trust God.

Chapter 9

The reason I was listening to my mentor was because she was going to the same addiction counselor, and he had helped me immensely.

It was the first time someone asked me questions about me, and my family and I wasn't afraid to tell the truth because there were no ulterior motives. He wasn't going to rip my family apart — truth be told, that had already happened. I didn't have to keep the family secret in hopes of saving us from the boogeyman.

The Counselor really cared about me and after a few sessions he cried and said to me, "Betty Jean, please don't take this the wrong way, but most women with your history become prostitutes on welfare. I am so proud of you. You will be OK."

That could have offended me, but it didn't because I was so happy, he believed in me. I heard his heart. That man saw me for months, free of charge, because the pastor at the church he counseled in had also heard a part of my story and agreed I needed help. Because I couldn't afford to pay the fee, again God had his hand on me. Tom became like a father figure to me. He was safe, concerned, and able to help me to see that I had suffered a lot of trauma and that there was hope if I just stayed clean, sober and away from men for a while. I needed to focus on me and not everyone else.

I started to feel again, something I hadn't done since I ate those three sandwiches at age nine. I will never forget the day when I walked into the massive church—the one where Tom worked and where pastor C. preached the good news for ragamuffins like me. I hadn't been in church since I was a missionary in upstate New York— almost five years earlier. I was alone (nothing new).   I wept. I cried endless tears — not of condemnation, but of conviction. I was so broken, so filled with shame, regret, guilt and disappointment at what I had become…. Who was I anymore?

But the songs washed over me like balm. I literally felt God singing over me. I felt his beautiful strong arms wrapped around me.   He wasn't disappointed in me. He was just so happy that I had come back to him.

It took weeks of walking into that church to stop crying like that, but it was necessary. Pain was inevitable. It was the suffering I put myself through that was optional. I could take a bat to myself relentlessly. I had to be reminded *often* that if God forgives me, it's OK for me to do the same.

The people in my new church were supportive, loving and kind. I got involved in the college and career group. Even though I had dropped out of college because of lack of money. I enjoyed the activities and fellowship.

I worked in the after-school program for minimum wage. My mentor reminded me that staying humble was important. I didn't need to work at the clubs making a lot of money bartending or serving alcohol. It was in my best interest, as well as others, to stay away from the temptations of my past. Being in my new safe environment, I had a much better shot at staying sober. I did just that— until — the day my parents came to visit me and my family.

I was in my grandmother's house visiting and my father was behind me. He patted my butt and said, "Nice ass Betty Jean."

I froze. It was the first time in years that I had not been high, drunk or stuffed on a food binge. I had about two months of being free from alcohol, but something snapped in me. I know now what I should have done, what I had learned by then. I should have called my mentor, Tom, my pastor or anyone who would listen. But instead, I called a drinking buddy and out I went to my old stomping grounds. I ordered a huge drink and drank it. I ordered another and as soon as I finished it, I realized I was done. Really done!

I wasn't going to hurt me anymore. I wasn't going to punish me for my dad's actions! It was the first time I had clarity. My father was sick. It wasn't normal to smack your daughter's butt and comment on it like he had. I had a flashback of other things that happened between us. In that moment my eyes were finally wide open. I had never been so sober in all my life. Even if I drank enough for a buzz, I picked up the telephone from the phone booth in the front of the restaurant and I called my mentor. I told her everything and for the first time ever, I told her the truth. She called our therapist Tom. She had been working in a local treatment center. I couldn't afford to go there, but together they got in touch with a place where they could send me on a scholarship. In a matter of minutes, I went from relapsing to overcoming. I was truly done…… I had hit my bottom.

I was on a train the next week headed for the most painful, eye opening twenty-eight days of my life. It was time for the truth, and nothing but the truth, so help me God. God's help I would surely need.

The intake lady asked me about a hundred questions, or at least it felt that way. I answered all of them truthfully. Thankfully, no one came to take me away to somewhere worse than here. Every answer I had seemed as though I was speaking about someone else's life. I had no feeling attached to my story. It was very matter of fact, and it took time to allow myself to attach any emotion to what had happened.

At least I was here now, and I was willing to tell her my story.

We had group counseling and we had sessions that included group reenactments of our families. I had a psychologist who, after seeing me a couple of times, told the nurses, "Do not give her any medication."

He told me I had trauma and that I was emotionally immature and passive aggressive. He prescribed biofeedback to me and vitamins and more therapy. I was relieved that I wasn't mentally ill like my mom and brother. I am not saying it is bad. It's a chemical imbalance, I just was so afraid he would say that I was. I didn't mind being emotionally ill and immature. Of course, how could I be anything else? I had stopped growing and maturing the day I ate anything I could get my hands on at the age of nine. It wasn't *what* I was eating, it was *what was eating me.*

And then to drink and drug at the age of eleven was why I was emotionally stunted. I never felt anything until the day that I broke down in church.

They probed me, and they exposed me. Not like the dancing did, but deeper. I confessed everything instead of being a Pollyanna show girl. I became a little girl again. A little 9-year-old girl who finally got to advocate for herself. I exposed my truth and it felt good. I felt validated. I felt free, and yes of course, I got angry for the first time ever. I learned it was OK to be angry and to be sad and to be real, but by telling on myself and on the others, I was becoming free. "The truth will set you free." I was on my way to becoming an eagle, not an injured pigeon. But all this takes time! Even diamonds go through a process. Due to the immense pressure that is present in the earth, as well as the extreme temperatures, a diamond gradually begins to form. The entire process takes 1 billion to 3.3 billion years. Obviously, it wouldn't take that long for me, but you can't put a clock on someone's recovery time.

I needed help. I needed space and I needed hours, weeks, months and years to stabilize. It wasn't an overnight matter. It has taken a lifetime to finally get here. It would take every single second that I needed to heal. I would have loved one of the pastors or elders to have laid hands on me and healed me instantly— like some of the stories in the Bible I read about. And, maybe, in some ways, that had happened because, here I was.

But most of my healing was and continues to be a process. When you are in a very dark room and you open the blinds too quickly, the light blinds your eyes. It's wise to raise them slowly so your eyes can slowly adjust. That has been my healing, slow and steady.

I believe, had the shades been opened too quickly, my truth would have been too much for me to handle. Had I seen too much, too soon, I believe I would have not been able to come to terms with my reality. My psyche could not have handled more. God only gives me what he knows I can process. So, God being the perfect gentleman He is, gave me the right teachers to expose the light and the reality, and then they showed me a different way. When the student is ready, the teacher appears. I was eager to learn and to be taught. I was finally ready to be honest, open minded, and willing. I was ready to grow up. I might have looked twenty-three, but inside, I was still just a child. I wanted to be an adult now. I came across as so confident, strong and in control, but deep down, I was full of hate towards myself. I know that, because I would have never treated my friends the way I treated me. I wouldn't have stuffed them with a whole pie until they were sick. I realized that I was cruel to me and that I had punished that little nine-year-old girl who had hoped she would finally be saved— only to be wrong and not believed, not helped, and not heard or valued.

I understand today that my mom was sick. She couldn't have done it any other way. Where would she have gone? She had no driver's license and no job. I'm sure her parents would have said. 'I'm not getting involved.'

What could my mother do if indeed she had admitted that my father was inappropriate to me and abusive to us? It was just easier for her to close her eyes and remain a team player with my father.

I understand that now, but at age nine and at twenty-three, it was a hard pill to swallow —like all the ones I took on her birthday in 1984... I was done hurting me with food and with the knife that I would use to cut and etch a cross into my left breast. I was done cutting myself to pieces with metal and with stinging words. I was no longer on an island alone, separated and different from everyone else. I was part of "now."

 I was no better nor no worse. I was just like everyone else here in this facility. We had all been rescued from the demons from hell. If you're going through hell, just keep walking— and walk I did. In fact, I started to feel a spring in my step. I even decided to start to slowly run.

It was time to leave my new protective haven. I spent the last night thinking about what I had learned. Alcohol is like a snake, — poisonous! Don't touch it! I had an allergy to alcohol. My brain was wired differently than someone who was not an alcoholic. I can drink tomorrow but not today. When I wake up it's tomorrow again. I started to apply that thinking to food as well. I could eat pecan pie, pizza or a bag of chips *tomorrow, just* not today. I can talk to that guy who keeps looking at me *tomorrow* just not today. I wanted to honor me, my mentor and God. The staff told us that only one out of 10 will make it from here going forward. I was outraged. "Speak life." I yelled. "We all will make it!' — and I meant it.

They smiled and said no, the reality is, only one of you will.

I promised myself that it would be me, all the while convinced it could be all of us. I was told if I put a fraction of effort into staying away from the first drink as I put into partying, I had a shot of succeeding.

A year later when I attended the alumni reunion of our class from my 28-day treatment, some had died while others had moved.   But most had fallen off the wagon.

I was wrong about all of us being able to make it. I so wanted to prove them wrong. But I was right about it being me! I stayed sober, clean, and out of a relationship in order to focus on me. It was exactly a year to the day that I was with no men.

I honored my mentors' strong suggestions of no men.

It was exactly a year and a day until I finally looked at a man again. He asked me out on his boat.   We enjoyed coffee and lunch.   Then, weeks later, there were weekend trips.   Within six months, we were going to Disney World, the Keys or anywhere else he suggested. We were having fun.

I had a sober relationship.   We went to meetings and he heard my story — and he stayed.

One day, as we got off the boat, he turned to me very matter of fact and said,

"You need an older man to take care of you and to marry you. I want to be that man. "

I was quite taken aback. I was twenty-four and he was thirty-four. He had wanted to be a bachelor, but upon meeting me, he changed his mind. He wanted to take care of me. I had always taken care of everyone else and now a man wanted to clothe me, love me and give me security. I may not have had butterflies or fireworks inside my belly, but I had gratitude that someone saw my value. That seemed quite desirable and so I said yes. We married without much talk about our future goals, but I was relieved he had accepted my past and humble present.

It was different having someone lead me. He worked hard and long hours, but we played just as hard on our weekend excursions. He bought me the model car that I saw at the car shop he worked in. It was a brand new white, Grand Prix with gold wheels and all the bells and whistles. I was ecstatic! We bought a condo in Boca Raton, which was temporary. We also bought a half acre in the Treasure Coast, an hour north of us, where we built my dream house. Pink, rose and white was my theme. There were a few chandeliers and the backyard had my dream pool and hot tub. We had closets as big as the one I had used as a bedroom in my last year of high school. The bathroom had marble floors and a jacuzzi big enough for two. I had arrived! I couldn't believe how one person caring for me could change my direction in life in a matter of days. It was mind boggling to me.

I enjoyed the meetings and my lifestyle— and not having to work anymore.

I went to classes to become a certified Personal Trainer. It was a dream for me, and I excelled. I took on home clients and worked a few hours a week. It was refreshing until the day he told me that his mentor of two years had lied to him... His mentor had taken his money that was for our condo and pocketed it. He was devastated, not just about the thousands of dollars that were stolen, but that the man he revealed his whole life to had betrayed him.

I couldn't blame my husband for being visibly affected, but he used this new revelation to choose not to continue going to the meetings and then he eventually completely shut down. He changed instantly.

Instead of going to an hour of solutions with me, he worked longer hours. He decided to go to school to become a paramedic and firefighter in the evenings while he continued working long hours at his family car service business. The responsibilities were huge. He and his brother took over their father's 35-year business. He was driving over 80 minutes away, to his car shop in south Florida. He worked eleven-hour days and then went to school immediately after for several hours.

In just a few months I went from being the "apple of his eye" to just another fruit on a tree — or at least that's how I felt.

He took us out often to eat on weekends and there were occasional weekend trips with our yearly Disney pass.   But basically, I was alone in my new house 90% of the time. I sat in my beautiful, lightly furnished living room on the rose plush carpet, patting my beautiful new Siberian Husky and said to God,

"God, I thank you for this beautiful house that you have given me, but it's not really a home."

I went to our bedroom and for some odd reason, went to his night stand and opened it. Inside lay magazines full of naked woman with breasts even larger than mine. I was devastated.   I had begged him at times to be more intimate with me, but once a week was all we had together.   I wanted him to desire me— to love me and hold me.   He said he had no time and no energy because of his full schedule.   I had reluctantly believed and accepted that until that moment.

I was sick.   I would have indulged his fantasies.   I would have happily delivered any sexual requests. He was my husband. It would not be just my duty, but my pleasure.   I wanted to please him, and I missed our intimacy.

Intimacy: Into me you see or into you I see.

Like me, he had his own closet full of skeletons. I tried, but he saw nothing wrong in our relationship the way it was.   But I was on an island once again and I knew I couldn't survive here alone.

He disclosed to me weeks later that he didn't think he could have children because of a football injury he had in high school. I wish he would have informed me prior, because I was trying to conceive in order to at least have a life and family while he was absent. I took my temperature, sought out a fertility specialist and even begged him to go to our second session together. The doctor stated that we would need to have sex more than 3 times a month which after two years is what was our norm. It was after we walked out of the Dr.'s office that he reluctantly disclosed that he was most likely unable to have children.

"Why didn't you tell me?" I asked with a heavy heart.

"Because I was afraid you wouldn't marry me."

That was unfair. Withholding was as much a lie as was a blatant untruth. My husband could not conceive and now he was gone except for the hours that we slept.

He no longer participated in all the recovery activities we used to be involved in. Now, instead of holding me, kissing me and whispering to me. " I will keep you safe and warm." He turned his back and coldly said, "It's not me. You are exaggerating. I'll see you in fifteen hours," and in the car he went with a magazine tucked inside his pants.

Chapter 10

Right about now I want to throw up. I want to close this damn notebook I'm writing in and cry my heart out. Maybe even just take a time out and come back to this another time. But I know I must continue telling you everything. I finally have the courage to tell it all, but it's painful. It hurts. I wish it would have ended differently. It could have been that I stayed, had three kids and lived happily ever after. But nope, that may be someone else's story, but it most certainly was not mine. Unfortunately, the damn onion I had started to peel was only a couple of layers down at this point. I had a jumbo Vidalia onion and many more layers needed to be shed before I even touched the core. I wasn't even halfway through.

I feel the need to apologize to you readers. Trust me, I'm over me too. I'm such a slow learner. If you are still with me, thank you. Thank you for staying on my journey. I need you. I am so grateful for your loyalty. I am in awe of you being loyal, something I had always been. It's bizarre how I could be loyal to my family of origin but now it wasn't as easy.

I left my husband and moved into my grand mom's place for a few weeks.

I had just met a man in Denny's on a Sunday morning two weeks before while on my way to church.

  My husband couldn't make it as he had on previous Sundays. So, I went without him —but not before a steaming hot cup of coffee.

A man came up to me and told me I was pretty. He handed me his card and when I told him I did personal training part time he exclaimed, "I need a trainer! I'm so out of shape! Please call me to schedule an appointment with you."

 It was innocent enough, so I assured him that I would call, and I stuck the card in my purse and forgot about it. The fact that he got into a BMW with his dog did not escape me.

He was tall and confident and from what I surmised, was out of my league.   He was a professional at a local hospital. I pulled the card out and exclaimed, "Why not? "

He was more attentive to me in the first five minutes than my own husband had been in five months.

 We talked for a few minutes and agreed to meet. I didn't leave my husband for this man. I was devastated about it, but I was able to somehow rationalize and justify that only days after leaving, that I needed some attention —someone to see my worth. And so, I exchanged my "pretty little life " of being cared for financially to being doted on physically and intimately.

75

The passion was beyond anything I had ever experienced. I was wowed when the daily cards were exchanged. I loved the flowers he gave me every week and the cute letters he wrote to me. I loved the constant compliments he showered me with. I was crazy in lust and almost in love.

I refused to get engaged at first, but I was happy to remove the big rock of a ring from my husband and replace it with a commitment ring. I was too scared to do anything more. I enjoyed us. He had an opportunity in New England. Although it had only been a few months, I jumped at the opportunity to go with him, even though I had not yet gotten divorced.

My husband in the meantime had also met a woman. But both of us continued to stay married to one another while living with someone else.

We only stayed together in the New England area for a couple of years when, one night getting out of his truck, I looked under his seat and saw a bunch of magazines. I questioned him, and he just looked down in embarrassment. He had about a hundred Victoria's Secret catalogs stuffed under the passenger side.

I was ill. He had heard my whole story about my husband and me and had assured me he would never do that. In fact, he would tell me again and again how gorgeous I was and that no other girl could ever take my place.

I threw the books down and walked up to our apartment, took my belongings, got into my Grand Prix and left.

"What the heck is going on? " I asked God.

I left my husband because I met someone who swore he would never dishonor me like that. Now I was all the way up here in Connecticut. At least my husband had given me security and more money. I reached out to him, but he was deeply involved and in love with this new woman.

I prayed, and I begged God to forgive me. I wanted to go back home to him, but it was over. I was at an all-time low.

 Again, it wouldn't be until many years later that he would come back into my life as a friend and apologize for his part. I apologized for being so emotionally needy. Now we are friends and forgave each other.

Thankfully, I stayed sober and I no longer used food to "fix" me or numb me, but I felt such sadness and disappointment and betrayal once again.

Only a few days later, I felt nauseous. I was pregnant. My God!   I had finally gotten pregnant and I had only been in this relationship for about two years.

I was devastated because I had just come to terms with my new place in life.   I left where I was working as a counselor after having worked with the company for five years and began work as a fitness director in a beautiful and secluded spa.

I was confused as to what I should do. I wanted the baby, but not with him. I wanted to work as the director at my new job, but how could I continue if I was going to have a child?

He begged me to go into the hospital and get tested, and yes, sure enough, I was almost ten weeks along. He begged me to come back to him. I resented him. He had already had a fling after our breakup... And me? ...I was carrying his child.

I went into the doctor's office with the intention of terminating the pregnancy only to discover that when the doctor examined me, I was already bleeding and in the process of miscarrying. I couldn't believe the timing and I was relieved. The girl who used to walk with pro-life signs at church was now relieved that I had lost the baby. When I explained what happened to him, he was downcast and crying and didn't believe me. He thought I had gone in and had an abortion.

I may have walked in for that reason, but I walked out because it was already gone. He didn't believe me, but it didn't matter in the end. It was the truth, and now I knew I had to get the hell out of Connecticut. I came back to Florida and moved into my grand moms again. It was temporary. This too shall pass I thought, but for the first time ever, I went into a severely dark place. If I'm honest with myself, it was a depression.

"Get up and read Isaiah 54."

"What?"

I came out of my slumber. I sat up in bed. It was 3 AM. I looked around, and I heard it loud and clear, a strong manly voice.

'I'm not reading the Bible at 3 AM. I'm going to bed,' I exclaimed to myself. And then I thought better of it. I had never heard a voice awaken me and tell me to read anything.

I opened the Bible, and as I read it, I was in tears.

'Shout for joy, o barren one, she who had not given birth, break forth into joyful shouting and rejoice. She who has not gone into labor, for the sons of the desolate one will be more numerous than that the sons of the married woman, says the Lord. Enlarge the site of your tent to make room for more children, stretch out the curtains of your dwellings, do not spare them, lengthen your tent ropes and make your pegs firm for you will spread out to the right and to the left, and your descendants will take possession of nations, and will inhabit deserted cities. Do not fear for you will not be put to shame. Do not feel humiliated or ashamed, for you will not be disgraced. For you will forget the shame of your youth, and you will no longer remember the disgrace of your widowhood. For your husband is your maker. (I lost it as I read that!)

I was feeling so much shame over being separated, and the divorce almost finalized, as my husband had filed weeks before. I had tried to conceive with my soon to be ex-husband for months. And now I felt embarrassed and looked down upon after leaving him and being childless.

(I continued to read like my life depended on it, and it did.)

" *The Lord of Hosts is his name and your Redeemer is the holy one of Israel, who is called the God of the whole earth. For the Lord has called you like a wife who has been abandoned, grieved in spirit, and like a wife married in her youth when she is later rejected and scorned says your God. For a brief moment I abandoned you, but with great compassion and mercy I will gather you to myself again in an outburst of wrath I hid my face from you for a moment, but with everlasting kindness I will have compassion on you says the Lord your Redeemer. For this is like the waters of Noah to me as I swore that the waters of Noah would not flood the earth again, in the same way I have sworn that I will not be angry with you, nor will I rebuke you. For the mountains may be removed and the hills my shake, but my loving kindness will not be shaken, says the Lord who has compassion on you. Oh, you afflicted storm tossed, and not comforted, listen carefully, I will set your stones and mortar and lay your foundations with sapphires. I will make your battlements of rubies, and your gates of shining stones, and all your barrier walls of precious stones. And all your sons will be disciples of the Lord, and great will be the wellbeing of your sons. You will be firmly established in righteousness. You will be far from oppression. For you will not fear, and from terror for it will not come near you. If anyone fiercely attacks you, it will not be from me. Whoever attacks you will fall because if you listen carefully, I have created the Smith who blows on the fire of coals and who produces a weapon for its purpose. And I have created the destroyer to inflict ruin (no weapon that is formed against you will succeed) and every tongue that rises against you in judgment you will condemn. This peace, righteousness, security and triumphs over opposition is the heritage of the servants of the Lord, and this is their vindication from me says the Lord. "*

I was balling hysterically, crying out to my God. I couldn't believe what I had just read. Every single word resonated with my broken heart. My soul was beyond tormented and here God woke me from my deep slumber to remind me once again that He loves me so much and that He missed me. He forgave me, and it was high time that I do the same.

I fell back asleep and awoke with a lighter heart and rested spirit.

I went back to work as a weight loss counselor and I once again committed my life to the Lord, just as I had as a child. I was reminded of the time my mentor asked me to write down a definition of God.

"He *is powerful, almighty, a friend, a father, a gentleman, majestic, just, loving, kind, giving, peaceful, strong, and holy.*"

When I had read it back to her, she said, "So why wouldn't you turn your will and your life over to Him if He is indeed all of this?"

 She was right. I had forgotten. I had a "built in forgetter" at times. Usually that happened when it came to the opposite sex.

 I was repentant and relieved to be back in sync with God. So many times, I had turned my back on Him. But deep down I knew that He was my only true hope. I would stand up for Him if I had to.

In fact, one time in my theatre class that I was taking at a local college (I had started attending again at age twenty-seven and I had switched my major from psychology to exercise science), the professor required me to say, "*Jesus Christ*" in vain during a monologue that was required. I told my professor I must respectfully decline.

"Why not?" he retorted.

"Because I don't say God's name in vain," I said politely.

"I will fail you if you don't comply" he spat.

I read the monologue aloud but skipped the Jesus Christ.

He grabbed my sheet of paper and put a big zero on it. After the class several students came up to me and said, "Wow. I respect your great faith. I don't know if I could have had the courage to do that. "

I thanked them. I got a grade of C instead of the A that I deserved. But I knew God was quite pleased, and so was I.

I had gone backwards, walked away, not put my trust completely in him at times, but I would not mock him. Jesus Christ was indeed my favorite person, my Savior, my best friend, a Jewish Carpenter, Rabbi, and my king of Kings. I wish I could have lived like I did in that moment, with conviction and standing tall for God.... Most times I had been. However, for some reason, I still tried to do relationships with men all on my own. Because of this, I suffered.

I was like an Indian giver with God at times.

'Here God I give you everything, '—only to take it back.

But still it was always the next guy I was attracted to.

At first, they seemed different from the prior relationships I'd had, but within months, the truth would come out.

Look, after I shared my story with my mentor, I realized I had plenty of weaknesses and character flaws, that I just plain missed the mark.

I realized my denial in life, my pride, my low self-esteem, my ego and fears, and my patterns with others, especially with men were a problem. I realized that I was a full-time job, emotionally. I was immature.

And not to keep pointing the fingers at others but what was my part? The common denominator in each relationship was me. Even with this newfound knowledge, I tried to do it on my own, once again.

'Here God, I've given you my alcohol, drugs, and food addiction, but don't worry I have the men Department. I can handle it from here.'

It's too bad I didn't give him that too. I would have spared myself the most exhausting next eighteen years of my life. I tried to keep myself in check. How was I doing? Was I making the effort to work on me? Was I getting the outcome from my higher power or trying to do it my way? I was vigilant about my side of the street. I had done a lot of harm, i.e. — the jobs I left without telling my bosses. My mentor encouraged me to put everything down on paper that I could think of, and I did. Then she said, "Put God *and* you on the very top of the list of people you have harmed."

I had done harm to many people, and I was eager to let them know how terribly sorry I was. My first fiancé wouldn't forgive me. I understood, though it still pains me. I even apologized to my parents for anytime I had been disrespectful or mean to them. I was truly sorry, and now it was time not to just to say it, but to change it.

I stayed in prayer and meditation. I had a much easier time talking to God. This stopping and listening was a struggle. I had been such a busy "human doing" now I wanted to be a good "human being" that took great effort. I was not comfortable at first being quiet and still, but practicing it was necessary. Progress— not perfection.

I was praying for God's will in my life. I surrounded myself with friends who were like minded, attended church, and read my Bible daily. I read spiritual books and I helped others by taking time to encourage and emotionally support them, just as I had been. I led meetings. I shared my experiences, strengths and hopes with my fellows. I had a spiritual awakening due to my changes. I tried to carry the message, and not my mess, to others.

I had a friend say his favorite sign was the exit sign. It's what you do daily out in the world in all our occurrences, whether it's to be nice to the cashier, smile at others, drive the speed limit or be kind and courteous. I started to get my conscious back and be a more mindful lady. The hardest thing for me is having a head full of truth, a heart full of God, and going against both. Doing the next right thing isn't always easy, but it's simple. Doing it does it. I can't close my eyes to the truth. Once I see the truth, I can't not see it. Once I hear it I can't not hear it. I learned that I can only do the best I can with the information that I have.

My biggest problem was I didn't wait long enough. I was still quite impulsive. It would take some more smacks to the head to figure that out. First there was relationship number two. The man who would give me my greatest gifts in the entire world. — *"Shout for joy, oh barren one, she who had not given birth, break forth into joyful shouting and rejoice, she who has not gone into labor. For the sons of the desolate one will be more numerous."*

Chapter 11

"I'm having friends over for dinner tonight, would you like to join us?"

Sure, I knew a few of the invited guests. We all went to the same self-help groups together.

I enjoyed his hospitality. His cooking skills were much better than my own. He really loved feeding me. I had grieved my first husband's divorce. I had put my first loss of the baby deep inside, but after five months I decided that I was ready to enjoy being around a man again. He was the most exciting, engaging and fun man that I had ever run into.

He had been a semi professional Hockey player in Rochester, NY. He took me to Panther hockey games, jet skiing, horseback riding, and there were power walks together every single morning. He was full of stories, full of life, and always ready for any kind of adventure. He would grab me, pick me up and carry me around like I was a queen. In fact, that's what he would call me, "His queen."

I had traveled many times to the East Coast, but with him it felt like it was my first time. He spared no expenses when he carted me off to the mountains in North Carolina. I loved it when he flew us out to

California, and we rented a convertible to drive up and down the Pacific coast highway. We stayed in Hiltons, Ritz Carlton's, and took limousines like we were celebrities. He showered me with both love and excitement. We went to shows like Grease, Crazy For You, and the comedy I love you, You're Perfect Now Change. We went to concerts such as Tina Turner, ZZ Top, Gloria Estefan, Phil Collins and Roger Waters. We were romantic and childlike every single day. He met my parents. He said he had never met anyone as sick or as crazy as my dad. But he stayed around anyway.

 He took me to his hometown in Canada to meet his best friends and his sister. We were very much in love. He expressed how much he had no desire to be married or to be a father. Despite that belief, he wanted to take me as his wife.

I told him in no uncertain terms that I would only marry him if we could have children. He agreed, and then just one year later, we would marry.

In that year, we continued to play hard. We served in our groups together. I got pregnant and miscarried. I got pregnant again, and again lost a baby. We were saddened. There was great loss for me, as now I had 3 miscarriages and I was heartbroken. I feared I wouldn't be able to carry to term. I was exhausted, as well as crushed. I gave up my hope and dream of becoming a mother. I was grieving my dream to become a mom. I even went back to a fertility specialist. They found nothing wrong but decided to shoot dye into my tubes to clear them just in case. Just when I had given into accepting, I would be childless, I found out I was pregnant again.

They shot progestogen in my butt as a precaution. We had only been married a few months, and I was six weeks pregnant. Honestly, I held my breath the first three months because I had lost the previous children at three months or less. I was so relieved when the doctor told me that the baby's heartbeat was strong and that the child was growing normally, and everything was OK. I couldn't believe I was having a baby. My new husband was so helpful. He fed me and took care of me. I continued to work as a weight loss counselor. I had top notch insurance. I had wonderful people in my life. My family was so happy for me. After years of trying to conceive, I was going to be a mommy. I sang songs. I read out loud. I prayed. I rubbed my stomach. We went to the doctor for my 4-and-a-half-month visit. I was told I was having a boy. I named him Tyler. His father rubbed Tyler and laughed when he saw his feet kicking my stomach. I was never so happy in all my life.

I devoted my son to God. I thanked God for my boy. He wasn't even outside of my womb, and I loved him fiercely. I ate healthy and I exercised, but I was extremely careful as I wanted him to survive, unlike the others.

My husband's mentor moved to Las Vegas, Nevada. He encouraged us to visit and check out a business we might be interested in buying. A friend of his was selling a huge landscaping business that served both commercial and residential customers. We were indeed, interested.

We had just bought and sold several condos. We restored and then sold them. We were financially secure enough to buy this fast-growing business in Las Vegas as the city was booming.

So, we purchased it.

My husband went out a month before Tyler was born. He found us a beautiful, brand-new apartment in Henderson, Nevada. It was small, but perfect to start. We planned on renting for six months and then buying a house when we got established and settled. Although I missed my husband that month, I enjoyed my pregnancy. I worked until I had about three weeks left in my third term. I napped for the very first time in my life. I would watch the TLC show, The Baby Story. I devoured books about pregnancy and babies. I enjoyed visiting my sister and friends. I went to Babies R Us and purchased everything I needed. Of course, the three baby showers that were thrown for me supplied most of my requests. I had many friends and family members that shared my excitement and blessed me with more than enough for our new addition. I glowed. My pregnancy was normal.

The day my water broke was quite difficult and even traumatic. The doctor was unavailable, and so they had someone else take her place. But the Dr. was already on an emergency C section. So, we were told by the nurse to keep Tyler from coming out, per Doctor's orders. I felt the urge to push for about 45 minutes. It had been thirteen hours of pain with no anesthesia. It was barbaric as far as I was concerned. After Tyler's head began to crown, I saw a woman (who ended up being a midwife) passing by my room.

I yelled out with a cry, "Please help me deliver my baby!"

She came in and did just that.

Within minutes he was in my arms, and I didn't exhale until I heard him scream, and cry. He was OK. Tyler was beautiful with his blue eyes looking into my blue eyes. I knew I had never loved like this. I would love him and give him the life I had always hoped for. I would protect him. I would nurture him. I would keep him safe from harm.

Tyler was always so strong. He excelled in everything. The books gave me time markers on when to expect him to lift his head, roll over, crawl, walk, talk, and such. Not only did he do things much quicker than expected, but he was eager to participate in every activity with gladness, and passion. I applauded every accomplishment and my husband was so helpful. He would help with the diaper changing and the early morning feedings. I breast fed for two months. It was my favorite time at night to sit in a rocking chair with Tyler. We were both in love with him. I call him my survivor. "Tyler, my survivor!" He was strong to be conceived and born. His strength was certainly something that has stayed with him his entire life.

Friday afternoons at 2 PM, my husband would pick us up from our new apartment in Nevada. We would religiously go to a matinee movie. Tyler would sleep beside us, and we could enjoy a date together. It was our ritual, —that and going out four times a week for dinner buffets.

We took Tyler everywhere —- California, Zion Park in Utah, the Grand Canyon in Arizona, and New Mexico. Tyler got to see most of the West coast from his car seat by the time he was nine months old. He even drove out to Nevada with us when we moved from Florida to Nevada, at the age of three weeks. We didn't let having a child slow us down. We continued to live life fully, and we had a blast.

It was Friday and I got Tyler fully dressed. We were ready to be picked up for our 2 o'clock movie. We waited. The second hand continued to move to the right, but my husband was not here. He was always early. I began to worry and called him. There was no answer. He always took my calls. I called again, but it went straight to voicemail. I called his best friend and mentor. He said he had no idea, but that he noticed he hadn't been hearing from him lately and that he hadn't seen him in his usual support group. He suggested I should call the hospitals, and the police. Now it was already three hours later. I did just that. He wasn't in the hospital, thankfully, and when I continued to try to reach him, I only got his voicemail.

The police came out to speak to me, and when they checked our home and his closest, they asked if he had a drug problem.

I told them he was a recovering addict.

"What drugs did he use?"

"I don't know," I said, but told them he had been clean for years.

They asked if he could have a girlfriend.

I gasped, "No! Of course, not," and then they left.

A few hours later, after midnight, he walked in looking like a corpse. His face was distorted. His eyes bulged, and his lips could hardly move. He apologized profusely. He couldn't talk much because his heart was racing. He was high.

I was horrified. I knew nothing about this drug he had used. We had a new baby. We lived in a new area. I was beside myself. I was angry.

I demanded, "How could you get high when we have such a beautiful child and life?"

I felt betrayed. He agreed to go back to his support group. He picked up a white chip and started over. It would only be a week before he would succumb to another slip. My new mentor that I found in our area suggested I go to a fellowship support group that could help me with similar situations. I did just that.

I found a lady there to mentor me as well. I was so dumbfounded and exasperated. My best friend, husband, and father of our new joy couldn't stay clean. My new support system said things that helped me to take the sting away. —I didn't cause him to use. —I can't cure him. — I certainly cannot change him. — He is sick, and not bad.

One day my mentor even explained to me, "Look, visualize that he is in a bathrobe with the thermometer in his mouth and slippers on his feet. He is sick. Get the chicken noodle soup ready."

Her point being that he wasn't evil, but rather that he was ill.

For the first time, I felt what it was like to be in the other seat.

I had been the struggling alcoholic in my past. I saw firsthand what it was like to be on the receiving end and I was devastated. Both were equally tormenting and heartbreaking. He would take off for hours and sometimes even a couple of days. I lost trust in him. He opened his mouth and the next story came out as to where he was or where he was going. I urged him to go back to Florida where we had a strong support system. He agreed. We went back home.

He was able to stay clean for about a month. One day, as we were on our way to a wedding, a woman was walking down the street, looking for her next client. I saw him eye her. I don't know where I got the next story from, but I told him I knew he had been with this type of woman back in Las Vegas. Sure, enough he put his head down and said yes. He was sorry. He promised he would stay clean and away from women, but it was an endless battle...... We separated, and then we got back together.... We purchased a home. He managed to stay clean for a couple of years.

I was grateful we were back to our old life. I conceived again. Dylan was born, and like Tyler, I was in love. I had two boys which are two years and ten months apart. Tyler wanted a little brother. I was so happy. Tyler was mesmerized by his brother.

At first, he loved him, but as the weeks went on, he became jealous of him, due to all the time that Dylan required. Dylan was colicky, just as Tyler had been, until he was four months old. It had taken a lot out of all of us trying to keep him comfortable and quiet.

We had a lovely college student living with us in our 4th bedroom to help us out part time. I had worked with her in the Country Club fitness center. I hosted meetings for new moms in my home. All was well again.

I started personal training again, only two clients per afternoon. This was enough to help with our health insurance. My husband took on a pool service business as well as buying, restoring, and selling houses again. We were doing well financially and were once again a family unit. We enjoyed our home. We had friends over to swim in our pool. We hosted barbecues, parties, and continued to travel as a family. We kept quite busy and enjoyed being parents of two little boys.

I loved my husband. I forgave him for using and for not being able to be loyal in our marriage. It was hard to trust him, and it affected me deep down. I wanted to stay married and to try to overcome our past. About 10 months later he said he wanted to get away alone. We had always done everything together— unless he was using drugs.

I begged him not to go, but he was determined to leave.

He got into his car and I ran after him with Dylan on one hip, and Tyler on the other. I dropped to my knees and cried out, "Please don't leave us!"

He sped off. It was the quietest three days I've ever had, — even if the boys were loud.

When he returned, he was quite beat up. His hair was matted, and he looked disheveled. He didn't think it was fair to me to go on like this and I agreed. I moved into the other bedroom. I apologized to our nanny who, after living a year with us, had to leave.

I began to pack slowly, not quickly like past times.

I asked if I could pick up extra shifts at work and they obliged. I went on an interview at another fitness center and I was hired by a woman who I respect and love dearly. She went above and beyond for me and my boys often. I was relieved I would be able to financially take care of my boys. After months of trying to no avail, I moved us out. Tyler was three and a half and Dylan was a year old. I was thirty-four.

We moved into a small two-bedroom apartment. It was a simple place— not like the big house we'd had with all the luxuries, but it was quiet, serene and it was absent of heated discussions about drugs and women.

I missed my husband, but not our crazy ups and downs. I had been on such a rollercoaster ride and I was tired of it. He would come back once again and asked me to try after I served him with divorce papers.
  But after all the broken promises, I had to take care of me and the boys. I was afraid they would be exposed to the wrong women and the drugs. For our own safety and wellbeing, I had to follow through. I divorced the man who fathered my children —the only man who had given me my greatest gifts. For that I would always and will always be grateful. I would have given my life to save him— to help him —to give him

my sobriety. But it doesn't work that way. It was a process to know deep down that we are only as well as the sick person in the relationship. Every time I put my hand out to pick him up, I went down instead. He wasn't bad... He was good. He loved me and he loved the boys.... He just couldn't say no to drugs and then to what always followed.

How could I compete with that? I wouldn't nor should I. I wasn't perfect, I became controlling at times. It always takes two to tangle. I became consumed with fixing and curing him. I had heard from someone that you can love someone to death. I didn't want to enable him and do that. I had to really let go and hope and pray that he would hit his bottom like I had hit my own.

I was on my own again now with two pairs of eyes looking to me. I could love them. I would protect them. I would feed, clothe and take care of them. I would sacrifice my life for them, and I did.

It was my duty and my pleasure. I was putting one foot in front of the other, one day at a time. Don't drink. Get together with others who are like minded. Ask God for help. Stay grateful. Help others, let go and let God help —this too shall pass. God won't give me more than I can handle. Trust God. Trust the process. Keep the hope. Keep the faith and it's going to be OK.

I had to cheer myself on —especially at night. I would read books to the boys, bathe them and then put them to bed. Then I would lie in my room and thank God for my babies. They were my world and I *would* break the chain. I did the best I could every single day. I took them to the park after work.   We went everywhere together.   It was just me —and the boys.

Chapter 12

I had a couple of boyfriends over the next seven years, but in the end, there was no one I would consider getting serious with. I enjoyed being a single mother, though it was extremely challenging most times— mainly financially.

My former husband tried to stay clean and do financially what he was court ordered to do, but his addiction took precedence over him and over his responsibilities. I knew he loved us. He just wasn't capable or equipped to do his legal share.

 I did try and took him to court three times. But in the end, even the judge said, "There's nothing other than continuing to jail him that I can do."

 He was self-employed so nothing could be garnished. I had to be self-supporting through my own contributions for most of the time. That was quite difficult. I would work all day and try to keep us financially secure. I wanted my sons to have a great life— better than mine. We lived a few years in a 2-bedroom apartment, and I made sure they got to play football, soccer and anything else they enjoyed. We went to the movies on Friday nights and instead of having cable, we went to the libraries and bookstores often. They loved to read, and they would become avid readers like their mom. We loved going to Chuckie Cheese, parks, fishing, beach, bowling and to the local YMCA. They were involved in every recreational sport as well as the Y summer camp.

I loved every moment with my two miracles. I wasn't the perfect mother, but I love them tremendously and every second that I wasn't training a client I came to pick them up from school and/or daycare and we enjoyed our precious time together. I never realized how much my own father had done until now. The car insurance, health insurance, electric, water, garbage, food, car, clothing and gas was so overwhelming. I, for the first time, felt great gratitude and respect for what my dad had done for my mom and our family. How the heck did you do it I thought. You don't realize how much someone sacrifices until it's your turn. But I liked being responsible and capable. Still, it was an awesome revelation to me that my father loved me and my family. I understood some of his frustrations now for the first time.

 I was now quite tired after a long day of work and doing it on my own — sometimes with just enough milk and bread to make ends meet.   But each day I made it.

Thankfully, my favorite clients, Bill and Jenn, had me train their sons and their father and mother. That brought in enough money for me to make it. On paper it wouldn't make sense how I could pay for everything living in Boca Raton, Florida as a personal trainer. Doing it as a single mom with two boys was no easy feat. But we made it and they were able to go to the best schools in my opinion. I researched the top elementary schools. The one I chose was by far my favorite. It was in a lottery system and, thankfully, the boys got accepted.

I smile even now with that blessing. We loved it there. The teachers were wonderful and nurturing and the boys learned Spanish, French, and mandarin. Not bad for kindergarten through fifth grade.

They had great friends and we had sleep overs, parties and lots of great fun.

I continued to travel with the boys, but not as far as California like we had in the past. But we would go to visit my youngest sister, Lisa, and my mom who moved to Michigan, and my brother who still lives in Pennsylvania. We went to places like Disney World, Busch Gardens and even spent time in cabins in Georgia and North Carolina where we loved the simplicity of a fireplace, rocking chairs and a hot tub on the wrap around porch. We loved to go and stay busy. We rarely stayed home. We were all buddies. We were a beautiful family.

They would see their dad when he was clean and available. At times they would even stay over a for a few nights. But when we saw that he couldn't say, "No," to his addiction he knew better than to keep the kids. I needed to protect them at all costs. Mainly he would see them for a few hours at a time. A lot of single moms choose to keep their kids 100% of the time. Understand that I *never* let them stay with him if there was danger. But I also wanted them to have their dad in their life. I couldn't imagine not allowing them to see him —although it was a constant juggling act. I loved my children more than I disliked their fathers' choices. I would try to stay neutral with the visits and not say anything negatively to them about their dad.

I decided to monitor, daily, whether they should see him or not. He was quite simple to figure out. He would want to come and see them when he had clean time and when he didn't, he wouldn't call or show up or follow through with promises. It broke my heart for him, for the boys, and for me. The boys quickly learned that daddy 'was not well and that we love him despite his sickness.' They took the good and prayed for him during the bad. It worked for us. I had to supervise most times, but I was glad that they had a dad and that he had not moved away or died of a heart attack or an overdose.

I went to meetings in the Church to keep me spiritually and emotionally fit. By now, I had about fifteen years of sobriety and I knew a little bit about what I needed to do and not to do. I had made a few not so great choices, but I was quite pleased about most of my decisions at this time.

I had a new mentor and friend Laurie, who was like a big sister to me. I saved enough money to pay for Tyler's prepaid college fund for a four-year University. I did a five-year payoff plan for Dylan's four-year University and a year to reside in a dorm as well.

With God's help and a great mitzvah (a good deed) from a fellow member in my fellowship, the boys were able to go to a luxurious summer camp in the Pocono Mountains for three weeks in the summer. They loved it and both boys attended every summer for the next eight years. It was the highlight of their year. Every year they thrived. They enjoyed their majors and minors and they would call me on Sundays to tell me, with excited voices, how much they loved the campers, counselors, director and all the exciting adventures they had. They both talked about the horseback riding, fishing and flying trapeze. They ate everything in sight. They were grateful to go, and I was in awe of the kindness that the owner and director had bestowed upon us. We were on a Scholarship and although it would require about three months of work for me it was worth every penny seeing their beaming faces in the pictures they sent to the parents. It was truly life changing for them. I had enjoyed my summer camps years before, but it wasn't nearly as fancy or as active or had as many choices. I wanted my boys to have the best and they did! I couldn't have been happier for them —the love kindness and generosity of others was overwhelming. I was especially grateful for my friend, Laurie, who bought the boys all their camp gear on the camp items list that was required. God had told me long ago, in the middle of the night, "And great will be the well-being of your sons".

 I took it literally and I was seeing God's promises being accomplished. I suited up and showed up for work every day; for my kids each afternoon and night. We struggled at times, but we always came through…. God always made a way. Looking back, it was a very stressful time, but also one of my favorite times. I was a single mom and my boys were my life. I hoped and prayed they would feel loved, safe, happy and at peace. I never wanted them to feel that deep sadness that I had experienced at their age. I tried to compensate for what I missed out on. I got to relive my childhood with them. It was healing at times. I may have gone overboard a few times because I felt so badly about their dad. I tried to be both mom and dad. I'm glad that I did what I had to, and I have no remorse or regrets. I did everything in my power to give my boys anything within reason. We didn't qualify for assistance because I made a bit too much, but we did qualify for health insurance and I was quite pleased when I could put my head on my pillow at night. I would feel my mouth curve into a smile knowing I had done well. After all, the two boys sleeping soundly in the other room proved it.

Some members of the Country Clubs where I worked would try to set me up with friends. I met a couple of very nice people, but I had learned by now not to even entertain the thought of someone in my life if I saw a red flag. Dishonesty was one of those flags and it didn't take as long to figure out who was needing to be rescued or fixed. Instead of investing years trying to take on a project, I listened to my gut and my intuition. I could discern these flags sooner as I became better. I did get hoodwinked a couple of times. In fact, I met a great man, who after eleven months of what I thought was passion, fun and love, hadn't disclosed to me that he had a chemical imbalance. It didn't come out until he decided to go off his medicine. He went from being calm, stable and sweet, to a totally different person and unstable in a matter of days. I couldn't believe I had been misled again. I had been here before. Alcohol, drugs, sex addiction, — just fill in the blank. I broke up with him and he made my life a nightmare. He sent me hundreds of texts, inappropriate emails and I truly felt threatened for me and my boys. I got a restraining order and thankfully, the judge agreed. I was relieved we were safe, but I was disappointed in me for once again being deceived. I should have known better I thought. How was I to know? I once again only went with the information I had at the time. It was at least better than years before and I didn't live with him or marry him. That was an improvement! Hey, I'll take it!

But the fear this caused me, led me to do something I had thought about, but never done before. I started to run a mile— then two miles —and then three weeks later, three miles. It took the edge off and was a healthy way to blow off my concern and fear. I took this opportunity to comfort myself instead of using food or anything else self-destructive. I began to seek out 5 K races. I decided to run a 5 K race for a local charity: Race for Faith. It would benefit the world vision children and the veterans. I loved the idea of being part of a "not for profit" run. It was a bucket list wish. After about three and a half weeks, I signed up and ran the race like my life depended on it. I loved the thrill of helping others and the way it made me feel. It was exhilarating — all the many people on my left and right running beside me. It felt like a team and I finished! I thanked God for helping me to do it. I was forty-four years old and running my first 5 K. I did another one a month later and then a third, another month later. As I was getting ready to leave the race, I heard the announcer call my name out— "Betty Jean, you are first in your age group."

I just about fell over. In the other two races, I left before they gave out awards. Unbeknownst to me, they had metals for first, second and third in each age group. Who knew? I was in my glory. I was running, having a blast and even being rewarded for it! I loved getting medals. I loved the hardware. I was hooked. I chose a 10K for AVDA next.

I did well. In fact, I started to run often and would enter races monthly. I placed in my respective age group most times. I even trained for a half marathon for a local police league. (PAL) Running and runners were my new hobby and passion. It certainly was a lot safer than relationships, —just saying.

The boys would come and cheer me on and a few times we even ran as a team. We placed second on Mother's Day. That was a highlight for me. We were a great team indeed. I felt strong, capable, and empowered — something that had taken me a long time to experience. I was on a runner's high and it felt terrific.

I know there were times I was using running to run away from feelings and from me, but most times I ran because I could, and I liked it. I ran back to back races on weekends and I cried with joy and gratitude every time I heard my name called for an award.

I'll never forget when I was in high school and my PE teacher was timing the 12-minute mile. Before we started, I asked her, "What do you think about when you run this one mile?"

She said, "Getting it over with! I hate running!"

We laughed. She asked, "What about you Betty Jean? What do you think about?"

I straightened up and with a big smile said, "I think about those that can't run; who can't walk; who are in a wheelchair; who are crippled; and I run for them."

She looked at me and stopped," Wow! You are a kind person."

I didn't run that one mile very well back then. My large breasts made it tough. I was overweight, but I ran with my heart, soul and mind — and for all the handicapped people on my mind. I did not realize back then that I was just as crippled emotionally as they were physically. Running gave me a purpose again and winning in my age group was addicting.

It started out innocently enough, but as a lot of things I tried, if it felt good, I wanted more. I was addicted to more, and more — of anything and everything.

After about 1000 runs and seventy races, five of them being half marathons, I began to have injuries. I believe God was trying to slow me down, — even a good thing can be abused. I felt powerful and strong when I ran and competed, but my body wasn't a child's. I was middle aged. I pushed myself to the limits which at first felt empowering, but eventually would lead to my demise. After my first injury, I slowed down just enough to feel again— to be still —to be quiet —to be available again— to my next husband— to my biggest addiction of all....

Chapter 13

I was talking to a friend in one of my groups at noon. I saw a man waiting around on the side, until we were through with our 10-minute conversation.
He waited ten minutes. *'Wow,'* I thought.

"Hi....I'd like to take you out for coffee and a motorcycle ride?"

 I had seen him on the beach once, just a few months ago and he had given me his card with his contact number. I had put it away in my car and thanked him. I knew him from the same circle of friends, but as much as I liked riding motorcycles from time to time with friends, he seemed a bit too intimidating to me. He was covered in tattoos and sported a goatee. He was not my usual type, so I never thought I'd say yes to him. But because I had accepted his friend request on social media and he seemed harmless enough, I said, "Sure!"

 His Harley was beautiful. The seat seemed meant for me. Holding him and feeling the wind in my hair was like magic. I felt the sun on my face and when we would put the ear plugs in our ears, we could hear the country love songs in unison. I would watch him watching me in the mirror. I fell in love instantly. All the hard work, counseling and self-help had paid off. I would love with abandon for the first time ever. I would give 100%. I would fall deeply in love and I would be the best partner ever! It was intense, and it was quick.

We went everywhere together and attended church every Sunday. We served together and we got involved with the church's motorcycle ministry. We rode with other couples and went out to eat afterwards. He was great to the boys. We went 4 wheeling in his Jeep —and all of us as a family would go to the shooting range. We went fishing together. We went to the beach. We were inseparable for a very intense but short 7 weeks. He took me to the beach before his Bible study. He dropped to his knees and asked me to be his wife.

Looking back now, I should have run. I was a great runner by then. But I was madly in love and blind as a bat. I had seen only beauty and possibilities and potential. I was always in love with potential.

The pastor was his best friend and he did our premarital counseling. I saw no red flags. If this was OK with his pastor, it was good enough for me. We remained pure for the first four months of our engagement. But just days before we said, 'I do,' I caved. We were close, but no cigar. At least we tried and we didn't move into his home until after the wedding.

Mentors Laurie and Mimi thought we were rushing it, and looking back, they were right. They had been such wonderful friends— insightful and part of my support from so many obstacles. But I told them I had this. I was smitten. I was on cloud nine. I hadn't felt like this since the boys' dad. I hadn't been this serious in nine years. I felt entitled. I wanted my boys to have a stable father figure and this man had about seventeen years of being involved in the Church. He was a Bible believing servant for God. He led Bible group studies. He even taught new believer's classes for about six years. This was the real deal. I would be equally yoked. It's baffling to me even now how delusional I can become when I am thinking with my heart and not my head. I want what I want when I want it. My friends and family and support system were happy that I was happy, but also voiced, 'What's the rush?'

 The rush was, I couldn't wait to spend the rest of my life with this man. I felt safe with him. We were one. We were giddy with love and gratitude. I was never so sure of anything in all my life. I was convinced that this was the man of my dreams and from February through August, he was. But like an intense flame that ignites rapidly and forcefully and ferociously, eventually it must fade, wither and die down.

113

Overnight, my sweet, loving, compatible husband became indifferent, nonchalant and unavailable. I didn't understand when he said he didn't want to be married anymore. We had just returned the night before from our postponed honeymoon, to Italy —the most romantic twelve days of my life.

The boys were at summer camp in the beautiful Pocono Mountains and they would return to us being separated. He had organized a few friends to move us out of his place within two days of returning from the most beautiful time of my existence. What?

"You must go. I don't want to be married. I will give you the money you will need for first, last, security and the deposit for FPL and water, but you must go now."

"Are you serious?"

I begged him. I literally got on my knees and begged him for hours. I cried. I pleaded. I felt like I was nine all over again —begging him not to reject me —not to abandon me. What had I done?

He said, "I'll take the blame."

I was in shock. I had been the one before to leave every single time, and now that it was me, I was paralyzed with fear. I was confused. Not even my mom's running and hopping from room to room could have muddled me as much. I was dazed, bewildered, disoriented, and I said, "You can't be serious. Please honey, what's wrong? I don't want to go."

"You must go!" and off I went to yet another home.

I called my girlfriends and they pulled together and even rented me a U haul. About twenty women came to my side. Most came to help me move and organize everything. And to hold me as I sobbed. I will never forget them. They fed me. They comforted me. I was inconsolable. My friend Mimi took me to the grocery store to buy food. I was in a state of shock. The boys would be back in just a day. How would I ever be able to explain this to them when I didn't even know how to process this myself. The man who became their step dad and friend had moved us out and wouldn't be there when they returned.

The first night when everyone left after helping me put everything in order, I went to put my pants on —or was I taking them off? I couldn't remember. For the first time in my life, I understood what I had heard others say hundreds of times —I didn't know if I was coming or going. I was totally befuddled.

I fell to the floor, prostrate, crying, screaming frantically. I was overwrought with emotion. I had never ever experienced these feelings before. Not even my own dad who had betrayed me, rejected me, choked me, who looked at me with those wild eyes; — it had never ever come close to this. I hadn't seen this one coming. I felt like I had been hit head on and I wanted to die. Should I jump in front of a train? *'Oh God why? Why Lord? This man is my husband. We are equally yoked. I love him. This is my spiritual leader and my everything.'*

I cried for hours. I sank deep into my mattress. How I slept is beyond me. It was a short few hours of relief, but when I awoke again to the nightmare of my reality, I knew I would need to be strong for my boys. They would be coming home in a few hours. *'God, please help me! God help them, God I am devastated, but my only hope is you. I need you I can't do this without you.'*

With the little strength I had left, I drove to the airport and embraced my boys harder than usual and longer than necessary. I don't know if I was holding them up or if they were holding me up, but the three of us were locked in an unbreakable circle again for the first time in what seemed like an eternity.

We walked from the baggage claim to the exit.

116

"Boys let's get into the car. We need to talk."

They were just as perplexed as I was. They too were stunned. The rest of the day we remained quiet, as if we had just attended a funeral— and in a sense, we had. We had just suffered the "death" of our newest family member. We were all just doing the best we could.

I tried to comfort them, but I was certainly not able to be my 'Pollyanna cheerleading' self. Still, I tried to keep us busy doing and going, but even I was too tired and affected to be able to function with my old coping skills. Even God rested on the seventh day. This was my seventh day. I needed rest. I needed a break. But I had to go on. I didn't even skip a day at work. I had to process this, so I told no one at work. I was mortified because instead of sharing my Italy trip with everyone, I had to keep it together and pretend it was fabulous. If I had even tried to articulate how I felt, and what had truly happened, I'd have lost it. I had to remain strong. I had to work. I had to provide for my boys again, — now more than ever.

My new townhouse had three bedrooms and was $200 more a month then what I had been paying. I had to keep my composure, survive, and provide for us again. I could do this. I knew how to survive. I knew how to go on.

I would leave work after my eight clients, come home and collapse. I was "Little Miss go here, go there" as I crashed and burned. I was going through the motions but inside I was being buried alive and the boys were silently trying to catch their breath. I always could be there for them but today I could hardly show up for me.

I felt bad, but I couldn't muster the strength for the three of us. I could hardly put on my 'face mask.' I tried to breathe, and I gasped, 'God help me. God help my boys,' was my new mantra, my new prayer. How could I have gotten here again? The irony and the sad part of it all is that he came back and left again... We would repeat this process four more times until it was finally over after a year of him vacillating and us feeling like it took a toll on us.

I was done. I swore off men for the rest of my life. I had hit my all-time bottom. Just like the alcohol, drugs and food, I was truly 100% done with picking another man. I gave up.... It was me and God and the boys from now on — and I accepted it. I would finally rely on God alone and I would take the next few years to learn to fall in love with God and with me. I would learn to know me— to like me. —I learned to find *me*.

I went to counseling every Monday for one to three hours with my beautiful new pastor/counselor and friend, Karen. I know it sounds extreme, but I hit a bottom like I had never hit before. I needed every moment with her to help me grieve and face the truth. She helped me through my grieving process and with acceptance of my new lot in life. She introduced me to an author, Brennan Manning and his books. I devoured his books. His words ministered to my heart and soul. I would sob as I read them daily.

She suggested that I also read William P. Young's book, *The Shack*. It was a book that helped me to heal. To see God as someone who was more relatable and not so serious. I started listening to Neil Young again and didn't feel guilty at all. God loves all types of music and people. We are all his kids. I wasn't so judgmental about people. It's not my business to be anyone's Holy Spirit. That's up to God, not me. I journaled; I wept; I prayed; I mourned. I knew it wouldn't be easy, but I had no idea it would be this difficult.

I was different now. I had become more reflective, quiet and humble. I dressed differently too— modest long dresses that were loose fitting. I only went to women's meetings. If a man looked my way, I would walk away and keep my head down. I attended church more often. After all, I didn't blame God. He didn't put a gun to my head and make me marry someone I had only dated for seventeen weeks. I began to look at me— not with a microscope, but with a realistic magnifying glass and mirror. What I saw was the truth. I had not taken my time. I hadn't even given us four seasons before I said yes. He too was human.

I'm not going to assassinate his character. Like all of us, he had his past. I just finally had to admit that my track record was quite predictable and that I had the need to do things differently. The men I chose needed to be fixed or rescued and it was that side of me that I needed to come to terms with. I seemed to always be needy. The need to figure it out— the need to be in control —the need to make it work— the need to make it right —the need to do anything at all was all my part. It was clear to me for the first time ever — crystal clear! It wasn't everyone else. It wasn't bad luck. It wasn't even that I kept picking losers! It was,' *Why did I think so little of myself? Why would I even consider being treated the way I had allowed myself to be treated*?'

I had a lot of unlearning to do and I had a lot of soul searching to attend to. Most importantly, I was finally ready.

I remained still and quiet. There would be no more running away, no more running in circles. I would continue to run my races, but not to the extent I had. I would run to maintain balance. I would stay present. I would listen to hear - to learn - and I would remain teachable. I didn't know all the answers and I didn't have to be Superwoman or Wonder Woman. I thought of strong people like, Mother Teresa, Edith Edger, Oprah and like my dear friends who loved me, Mimi, Jenn and Laurie. I had been humbled. I learned that I couldn't always trust people or even myself and my great intentions...No, I could only trust God and God alone. He never told me to trust others. God himself in His word said, "Trust in the Lord, "—not trust in man or woman or me. He told us to *love* others not to trust them.

I could pray for people and have compassion. I could be kind and even forgive people. I wasn't condoning or saying it was right what they did. It didn't mean I had to trust them or marry them. I didn't even have to date them.... Imagine that! In fact, I didn't even have to spend time with them. I could be free from having to be the one that needed to find a man who hadn't been loved or appreciated. I did not have to give him what he missed. I didn't have to come in and save the day or to show him love for the first time or fulfill what he lacked. No! I looked to me and realized that I deserved it. I needed it just as much if not more. I would no longer put my life at the altar. I would be kind to me. I would be worth the sacrifice. God said it best, "Love your neighbor as yourself."

That implies that I loved myself already. Well, it was high time that I accepted it. If God says it, that settled it! So that was what I decided to do. I devoted all my energy and time to discovering *me*. It was about time. Finally, after all the self-help and self-care, it was time to have a romance with me! I believe that God danced a happy dance. I could feel his love cascade and flood over me. I could hear him sing over me. My eyes were on Him again and Him alone. Men had failed me... I had failed me .... I had failed many people as well, but God had never failed me! He never gave up on me. He never left me. He never abandoned me, and he never rejected me. We all are fallible. We all are human, and we all make mistakes. But God, in his tender and powerful voice, spoke to me in a way I will never forget. I could hear it as clear as a bell — just like my 3 AM Isaiah 54 moment. I have never been the same since that moment. How could I be? I was loved.

Chapter 14

I'm reading another Brennan Manning book. I am at the beach and listening to the rolling waves. I feel the warm sun on my face as the question the author poses is very thought provoking.

After reading his first two books, *Ragamuffin* and *Abba's Child*, he had my undivided attention.

'Imagine right this moment that Jesus walks in the door, comes up to you, looks you squarely in the eye, and calls you by one word. What is that word? What is the word that God knows you by— that is the entire sum of God's knowledge of you in His relationship to you? It defines your whole being. Is it a condemnatory word, a judging word, a congratulatory word, a word of affection?'

"To those who prove victorious I will give a white stone with a new name written on it" Revelation 2:17JB."

'Now imagine that the human person who loves you and knows you— knows more about you than anyone else in the world, does the same thing. This person is known to you by the constancy of his or her relationship to you. Through thick or thin he or she has stuck by you, though this faithfulness has often been tested. When that person says the word by which he or she knows you, what is it? Is it the same word by which Jesus knows you?' (Brennan Manning, *The Relentless Tenderness of Jesus*).

I sat for a moment contemplating that name, and what I heard was— Beloved Daughter.
As I repeated the new name, I heard God say, 'Yes! *Now say it slower Betty Jean. Say it again, but slower. Be loved daughter.'* I said it again but even slower.......
Be Loved Daughter....... I must have repeated it ten times through my tears. I felt God's unconditional, validating, merciful love cascading and washing over me like I was a newborn child. All my sins were washed away...

 All these years I had not been punished for my sins, but *by* my sins and my consequences. I had chosen a hundred times to do it my way. Here I was for the first time in my life, allowing God to really love me. I hadn't realized how often I had performed for him and others. Always trying to be a "good girl— A God girl." I looked for his approval— for your approval. I looked for anyone to applaud me— to validate me. I had needed someone to tell me that I was OK— that I was valued. Here I sat with God's love beaming and shining on me. He loved me not because of what I did for him or didn't do for him. He loves me in spite of what I do! He loves me because of who He is, not because of anything I could ever achieve or do. I realized that I wanted to please God and the fact that I wanted to do that, pleases Him.   God likes me. He is fond of me. He is crazy about me. He cannot keep his eyes off me.

I felt such gratitude and relief. My eyes have been opened by this realization and truth. I had heard it repeatedly— that God loves me. I had sung songs often that had to do with his great love, but until I could internalize it and personalize it and really believe it, it was just a nice concept and notion.
Now suddenly, it was as real as the sand on my feet. I felt like a school girl. I was loved by my ABBA father.

Abba Father, I belong to you. Me, your Beloved Daughter, Betty Jean.

Instead of the heaviness I had carried, I felt lighter. I treated myself differently now. I was kinder to me. I didn't have to **do** anything. I got to do what I wanted, — but not out of obligation or performance. If I wanted to go for a run, I did. I didn't need to run until I fell over from fatigue or run through an injury. I had a smile from deep within, not the plastered one I had learned to muster. I had an assurance that God's radical, fierce, and tender love was all I needed, and in turn, I could do the same for me.

I enjoyed traveling again as well going to the theater, hockey games, etc. I have been blessed with many clients and friends (especially Jenn & Bill) who continued to bless the boys and me with tickets for Panther games and Miami football games. Another sweet friend gave me Andre Bocelli box seats. If my clients could not make their events, they generously gave me the most amazing gifts to enjoy for so many venues. These included: Barry Manilow, Kenny Rogers, Paul Anka, The Blue Man Group, Fiddler on the Roof, A Bronx Tale, Billy Idol, Avenue Q, Moving out, Cats, and Annie. I also received Sarah Brightman tickets for my birthday gift. She is a favorite singer and performer of mine.

My boys were so happy to get to do so many things with me. I did not have a lot of extra money. We lived well but within our means. Both Tyler and Dylan also took piano lessons, and to this day, they both enjoy playing. The boys liked middle school but loved their high school. Tyler was a high school football player. In fact, he was "offensive lineman of the year" as a senior. He was awarded an amazing trophy. He was offered several divisions 3 school scholarships but decided to decline. After a starring role in his high school theater musical production, *Rock of Ages*, he felt that entertaining was his calling. He has been pursuing that as well as working full time.

Dylan is thriving in his Law and History Academy. He loves to debate. I think he will do exceptionally well, unlike his mother who loses every time I open my mouth. He is a natural. I love Dylan and our times together. He makes me a better human being. He challenges me to learn and educate myself about topics I am not knowledgeable of. He is a bright boy and literally brightens my day. I am proud of him. I am grateful that whatever the boys decide to do, they have options. One being the prepaid college plan I have purchased. Whatever they choose, I want to cheer them on. I want to rally behind them. I will always love and be here for them. They light my life up so very much. I have learned that my dad loved me. Being a parent is on a need to know basis sometimes. You cannot possibly know it all. My mother raised five beautiful kids. We at least had each other.

I was independent, strong, and capable because of my upbringing. I can now thank my parents for who they were, and what they provided. I can look back and although I can't change what happened, I can see it differently —with a new pair of glasses. I could see, understand, and have a new perspective. I have a new attitude about how I view my past.
I wasn't a victim. I was a victor. I wasn't just a traumatized little girl. I had prevailed. I had survived. I had endured. There were times when I felt like one of those blow up inflatable clown bop bags. I would be punched to the ground and pop right back up. At least I never stayed down.

I saw so many people around me go through similar situations. Some died when they couldn't take the pain. Some overdosed. Some sank deeply into depression, and others would end up hospitalized or institutionalized.

I understood. I tried to give back by speaking my story and mentoring other women. My testimony is not so different from yours or theirs. At the end of the day, we all bleed red, and we all breathe the same air. In fact, my first breath in this world was from God, and the last one I breathe will be with God here on earth. He is our oxygen. It is the same for all of us. So, let's just be kind to each other.... After all, we are all just walking each other back home to God.

 I have written my story a few times, but until now I did not feel worthy enough to share it. I am important, but 'not look at me important, I'm something else important.' I'm: 'Hey look at what God can do in me, for me, and through me, important.'

God took a ragamuffin and gave me the strength to walk tall in His capable and competent arms. Hand in hand we walk. Apart from Him, I am nothing. I am forever grateful that at the age of nine, I prayed that prayer, 'If *you're real God, tell my mum mum to call out for David.* '

I can still hear her calling his name now, *'David come here. '*

And God does the same for me. 'Betty *Jean come here.'*

I come. I don't look back. I am a step away, and I stay. I don't need to walk away, run away, or turn away. I stay. Trauma makes you go to faraway places. But now I can stay. I feel everything. God gives me the ability to feel. I do not have to freeze, fight, or take flight. I can stop, stay and surrender. God has me. I feel his embrace. So, I lean into Him.

When I had been sober for about 3 years, I had flashbacks. My body had memories of myself as a child. It was suggested that I go to my second treatment center for codependency, food, and sexual abuse issues. I learned there that I had indeed been traumatized. Trauma is real. I didn't even understand until recently how certain people, places, and things could trigger me.

For instance, violent movies or someone putting their hands towards my face would cause me to flinch. Someone scaring me just for fun would startle me more than it should. I still need to lock my bedroom door at nights to feel safe. If a man looked at another woman in my presence, I would flip out because of how my dad and my former husband had looked at other women. It terrified me that they would have abandoned me for someone else. The smell of onions on someone's breath could remind me of my dad because my father would French kiss me and he always ate onions. Being alone with a lot of men would make me feel uncomfortable. If a man lied to me, that would trigger something in me, and I would lose hours from panicking. When I am stressed or feeling unsettled, I can still have nightmares and night terrors.

I knew intellectually that I might be exaggerating or oversensitive. I had every right to be upset, but I would feel re-traumatized. It has taken a lot of discipline to overcome this way of thinking and feeling. I had to accept that I was indeed affected. I needed to be patient with myself, using meditation and grounding myself. I would look for three colors around me. I would listen for three different sounds. I can smell something like a flower or lavender or something to refresh my senses that will comfort and keep me calm. I can make a cup of herbal tea, take a soothing bath, go into nature for a walk or sit by the beach and just breath. I can keep gum or a hard piece of candy in my purse to use my sense of taste. I can go to my favorite deli and order Matzo ball soup and allow it to nourish and nurture me. I would repeat to myself: 'There is nothing I need to do. It isn't happening now. I can tell my mind to stop. It is only in my mind.'

I had to calm myself down when I had been re-triggered. I would reassure myself with this mantra: I know I survived because I am here. I did get away. I got away. I am safe. You are not my father (whoever triggered me). I belong to God. God stay with me. That trauma is in the past. I am having a memory. It is not happening now. I am remembering my trauma. I am remembering what happened to me with my dad. I'm remembering the man that molested me, and the man in college who had taken me back to his place without my permission and sodomized me without my consent. It hasn't happened in a long time. It was horrendous, and it is awful to remember. I am glad it is only a memory and no longer happening. I am afraid. I am having these symptoms because I am remembering the assault. I am safe. I am having a flashback. I am not in any danger. This is not happening now.

It has taken time to overcome my childhood as well as my adulthood choices. I wanted to survive and overcome. I must still be vigilant. I wish I could be 100% cured, but I was never promised a perfect or easy life. That will be when I meet Jesus in heaven. I am home away from home here on earth right now, but I am not alone.

I have my support system, my friends, family and my dog Cinnamon whom we rescued. I sometimes feel she has rescued us. She sure has heard it all from me. There were many times I laid next to her sobbing and she just stayed close to me and listened.

131

I am grateful for those twenty-eight days in my second treatment center where I discovered I had trauma— and it all started to finally make sense. It was what gave me the clarity to stop using food to punish myself; to keep others away; to protect myself from men and from participating in my own life. How could I go out when I was too full to move or too self-conscious to be outside of my bedroom.

I have spent a lifetime trying to put together all the pieces of this puzzle that I call 'me.'
I am resigned. I have not given up or quit. I have just given into the labeling and figuring it out and trying to make sense of every little detail. I have no idea what the plan is, but because I know the planner, I trust Him. Of course, I need to suit up, show up, and be available to myself and others. I am in awe of how much better God does for me than I ever could do for myself. God does for me what I could never do for myself. How do I know? I finally let him.

After reading every Brennen Manning book, journaling, counseling, massages, acupuncture, long runs in the parks and by the beach, I have accepted the losses in my past. I have gone through the grieving process of each, and every relationship including myself. I have begun the greatest affair with me. I was enough. God and I were more than enough.

I was a greeter at my church. I was training for an Ultramarathon. Unfortunately, I was injured after a nineteen-mile run. I hadn't seen the giant hole hidden by the grass, and I caught myself as I ran down the steep hill. It was time to rest. It was time to stop. Although I was disappointed, I knew well enough by now not to question God. He wanted me to be in a season of rest. I listened.

Dylan had a head injury from play wrestling with his brother. It was horrifying, as it changed Dylan's lifestyle. He needed to step away from modeling and He could no longer play sports, which he loved. The injury affected his memory and cognitive skills. He had to rest and heal as well. Their dad had gotten into trouble and had to go away to jail. I was hurting. I knew God was with me, but I was hurting just the same.

In church that Wednesday night, I asked for prayer by a gentleman who was part of the prayer group for new believers and greeting ministries. I was desperate for some healing for my family. Dylan had walked into the church kitchen as I asked for prayer even though he was supposed to be across the street at the youth group center. So together the three of us prayed. Dylan looked up after we said: 'Amen,' and for the first time in two years he looked comfortable with a man. He was leaning in, and wide eyed. His former step dad leaving us made him cautious and on guard. He was quite right in feeling this way. I had tears falling down my cheeks as I witnessed the kind gesture and exchange. I thanked the gentleman for his time and beautiful heartfelt prayer. I walked into the service a bit more peaceful, relaxed and relieved.

A few days later, the church hosted a picnic for all the volunteers. I brought the boys along with me. Tyler rode his bicycle to work that morning and he wanted to leave it at work and retrieve the bicycle after the picnic. I went to sit at a picnic bench alone, as the boys were involved in a game of kickball. As I sat down, the man who prayed for us called out, "Hey no one sits alone, come and join us."

I recognized the others around the table, and instead of declining, as I had to all the other men in recent months, I walked over and sat down.

"Thank you." I said.

I enjoyed the company and the food. After a few hours, it became time to leave. Tyler asked me if we could ask if anyone had a truck. He was too tired to ride his bicycle back home after the picnic. I asked the group if anyone had a truck to help us transport Tyler's large bicycle. Marc answered and said. "No, I do not have a truck, but I can get it into my car trunk."

My trunk was full of exercise equipment I used for my home clients.

"Really? Thank you. "

Marc followed us to my work place and placed the bike in his trunk without any trouble and followed me home to drop it off. It did not even cross my mind to do what I had done in the past, which was not allow a man to see where we lived. I would have had him drop us off a block away from our respective townhouse. I was protective of the boys —more now than ever.

Although we were social, when it came to my residence, I was very private. But somehow it felt natural to allow Marc to come in for a cup of coffee. He had been one of the few people I had seen greeting people at the front door of the church who hadn't crossed any of my boundaries. He was friendly, but not invasive. I had seen him, helping in many capacities for the last year. But because I was still in my grieving process, I never even thought twice about him. After we had our coffee, Tyler wanted to go to the pet store with his good friend. I was in a dilemma as I was supposed to go to support my friend for her very first 5 k race. I could not be in both places. Marc offered to take my son and his friend to the pet store. I was at first hesitant, but both boys were high school football players and they both wanted to go. So, I agreed and allowed Marc to take them. He brought them back home within 45 minutes, safe and sound.

A few nights later Marc called and invited us to come to his home bible study that was open to everyone. We accepted his kind invitation and I saw many people from the picnic there. He was hospitable, and a good teacher with a great heart for God. Marc shared with us that he grew up Jewish and that he had his Bar Mitzvah at age 13. He shared with us that night that he was a completed Jew. He asked Jesus into his heart and life. He explained what a completed Jew is. I had never heard that term before. I had heard about Messianic Jews, but he explained that he had many experiences that led him to accept Jesus as his Messiah. I was intrigued and happy for him. I had always had a fond place in my heart for the Jewish people. Most of my clients and friends were of the Jewish faith.

When I watched the movie Schindler's list and the diary of Anne Frank on stage twenty-five years ago, it revealed what happened to the 6,000,000 Jews and I was shaken by what I had learned watching the movie and theater production. I felt a deep compassion and then a need to embrace the Jewish people who have been traumatized and unfairly slaughtered. I know I don't have any idea what they experienced... I would never in a hundred years compare my trauma to theirs, but as my Jewish friends would say, "Betty Jean, you had your own kind of trauma."

 I certainly am never going to compare the two. My pain is mine, but I just know that the pain in me wanted to heal the pain in my Jewish friends. Especially those I met who would reveal a number tattooed on their body's. Just thinking about it, I well up.

I remember watching the TV series *Roots* when I was a little girl. I remember after watching the series, that my love for my brothers and sisters that were black became even stronger. I hate prejudice. My heart goes out to anyone and everyone who has experienced prejudice. God says that we are all created equal. God said it. That settles it. The end.

 So, when Marc told me a little about himself, I was curious. He was mild mannered, soft spoken and wasn't in a hurry.

I had been used to being around aggressive, fast paced people. Marc had a free spirit and an easy-going personality.   After the Bible study, the boys and I quickly exited the house. It was a nice time, but I had to get the boys home and I wanted to be the first to leave.

A few days later Marc reached out to me and invited us over for dinner and a game night. We played some card games and laughed quite a bit. It was nice to have a friend of the opposite sex. It was a rarity for me.
The boys agreed he was nice company and it was refreshing after two years of always being on guard.

A few nights later, Marc called and asked if we would like to go bowling. I said sure, but after we hung up the phone I realized: 'I think he might like me, and I only want to be his friend.'

I didn't want to give him a mixed message and I was not ready to be anything more since I was still trying to come to terms with my last loss.

I called him back and apologized. I said, "I would prefer to keep our relationship within the church group, and I need to decline."

He was understanding and said, "OK" and when we hung up, I breathed a sigh of relief. I needed time. In one of my ladies' Bible studies, I remembered the teacher saying: "Go slow. Stay in groups and learn to guard your heart and body."

After all these years of giving God everything except my relationships to men, I was not interested in doing it my way again. I was done treating my life like a smorgasbord buffet: 'Here God, here is 80% of me and I will take that and leave the rest for you.'

No, this wasn't a salad bar where I would pick and choose what I would take and leave. I was willing to give him all of me once and for all. So, when I walked away from the phone, I felt pleased with myself.   It had taken me long enough.

But it takes what it takes and not a minute shorter and not a minute longer.

I went on with my day. I laced up my pink sneakers and went out for a little run. I blasted my songs and smiled a little more than usual telling God how grateful I was to be able to say no.

No— was a complete sentence. It felt good to say it and in doing so, I was finally saying, *Yes,* to me and to my Abba.   I was proclaiming that He was more than enough for me today.

That God and parent sized hole was the shape of a piece of pecan pie, a size of a tall alcoholic drink or the size of a 5 foot10 inch brunette. But not today…. Today I had been filled up by God himself and I felt full. I felt amazing and satiated. I needed this season in my life. The last two years had been my grieving time and I needed to be quiet. Even Jesus went up on to the mountain from the business of life and prayed to God. I relished this time "up on the mountain".

During those two years I continued to take care of my outside. I always enjoyed getting massages, manicures, pedicures and facials, but the one thing I had not mastered until now, was pausing, resting and stopping. Even when I drove, I would 'yield' at a stop sign instead of coming to a full stop.   I was always in a hurry. It took the same police officer pulling me over for speeding and then another policeman giving me a warning for not stopping completely to realize that I needed to be more mindful.

Now was my time to obey the law... stop at a stop sign, slow at a yellow light and do the speed limit.   All my life I had been rushing and racing through each task. There was always a "to do" list every day that would challenge me.   The problem was, I never celebrated the ones I checked off because I was always rushing on to the next list.

Now I learned to stop. The beach and the mountains were my favorite places to go.   I could enjoy nature, the waves and the birds. I loved hearing the birds sing. It was a far cry from when they would wake me up early in the morning when I was hungover from alcohol or food. Now I could rejoice when I heard them wake me in the morning, —It was, "Good morning God!" instead of "Good God it's morning!" That's funny and that too was changing for me. I could laugh again. I love laughing, comedies and musicals. Entertainers were always fun for me. I wanted to make up for all the tears.

I continued to travel. In fact, at this point, I had traveled to about thirty-seven of the fifty states. My goal was to see all fifty states by the time I was fifty-five and I was well on my way. I even decided to get a motorcycle license. I had loved riding and I missed it terribly, but I would not be at the mercy of a man in order to ride. Although I loved being on the back seat of a motorcycle, I wasn't going to set myself up again. So, I took a motorcycle class one weekend and then took the test. I passed it with a great score and out on the Harley I went. I couldn't believe I could rent a bike and ride. I was beyond pleased with myself. I was depending on God and on me and I was doing just fine. I also maintained my 5 K races on the weekends. I worked longer hours to provide for the boys and me and I was in a great place spiritually, emotionally, mentally and even financially. All was well with my soul.

I was walking into the grocery store when my phone rang, and I answered.

"Hi Betty Jean. There are a group of us from church that are going to another church on Friday night for a praise and worship concert. There is a man who will be leading it who has the gift of prophecy. Would you like to join us?"

Wow. It was Marc. I hadn't expected to hear from him again. I figured he wouldn't be interested in me after my request to only see him with the church group and I had forgotten all about him in the last week. But when I heard his voice and his eagerness, I was impressed by the fact that he had heard me. He had listened. He had honored my request and respected what I asked of him.

I was in awe of Marc hearing me.

I accepted his invitation and that night he picked me up. There were some other couples and a few singles that had come as well. We enjoyed the night. Afterwards, the prophet invited us to come up and be prayed over but I was going to leave when I saw the long line; but I decided to stay and waited to go up. It wasn't everyday someone wanted to pray and say a word over me. In fact, it would be my first time to have that happen.   I was usually the one praying over someone. I wanted a turn now.

 As we waited, we closed our eyes and listened to the beautiful soothing music. Minutes passed. I opened my eyes and when I looked to my right, everyone in our group had left. Marc looked at me and we smiled and then we laughed.   We each sank deep into our chairs and just enjoyed that moment. The line had shortened, and we went up individually.   When the pastor started to pray, I caught my breath.

"You love God," he said. "Wow. You love him so much, and you are fragile."
 And then he looked at me with both authority and compassion and said, "But no more counterfeit relationships!"

 My legs buckled. Just that week in my counseling session, I had heard that very thing.   That a couple of my previous relationships were counterfeit. My goodness! This man was from California and he didn't even know my name.   Yet he had read me in less than a minute,,,,,, *No more counterfeit relationships.*

 I went and sat down and sobbed. No more cheap, deceptive, fraudulent knock off relationships! I was done, and truth be told, I had never been so wide awake.   I was looking to fix, rescue and help heal all that in others, but I never realized that it was *me* that needed to be attended to for the very same thing. You spot it? You've got it.

I could glamorize my denial. Sure, I was trying to keep everyone from knowing my truth, my past, my life, — but in doing so, I was just projecting a knock off life. What you see isn't what you always get. My heart was in the right place. I wasn't bad. In fact, I was good. I was just broken and like Humpty Dumpty, I needed some more restoration. But not for a large audience anymore — now it was an audience of two — me and God.

I left that night spent emotionally, but peacefully silenced. I went to bed and I slept like a baby. I was grateful that my friend, Marc, was so patient with me. He didn't call until a few days later. He was having his pastor friend and his wife over for dinner and he asked if I would like to join them?

That was sweet. He was a good soul and I accepted his invitation.

His culinary skills were over the top and he would not allow me to clean up either. Before I left, the pastor that he had invited told us his marriage story and how he had met his wife. I was intrigued. It was a great story. But I wondered why he would be telling us about this since I was just friends with Marc.

I enjoyed the few hours we had together, and I said goodbye to Marc and his company. As Marc's track record would have it, I got a call asking if I'd like to join him again with another pastor friend of his and his wife. I smiled through the line as I answered "Yes!"

I was quite awestruck that Marc went to such great lengths to find groups of people to join us. I respected and admired him for his consideration of what I had requested. He respected me enough to not just acknowledge what I requested but to also comply with it.
I was valuable enough to him that he wanted to meet my request and I was moved.
I could admit then I hadn't thought much of me for a very long time. That was evident and probably more obvious to others than to even me. It pains me that it took so long to figure it out, but I also know many people it took until their deathbed to admit complete defeat.

Yes, I'm no spring chicken. I'm middle aged and halfway through my life, but I'm not dead yet. I plan on making it up to myself from here on out.

Dinner was fun, and his friends were quite charismatic and joyful, and the dinner was mouthwatering. I was enjoying our group outings and I was enjoying our slowly growing friendship.

One Wednesday night, after greeting people at the church, it was time to leave. Marc came to me and asked if I was hungry. There were no refreshments left and I was starving. I had just finished running about ten miles that day. I called my Counselor Karen, who was now my friend as well, and she said, "Betty Jean, he has heard your boundaries and he has complied with all of them. He has shown you he is a gentleman and that he cares about you. You have taken your time in the last six weeks and he has been respectful. He is asking you to go out to dinner— not to marry him!"

"Ha! Ha! Ha! " I laughed. "I know. I just want to be accountable to you."

"Go have fun and enjoy your dinner," she said, and we did.

When we looked at the menu, he suggested I get the Chilean Sea Bass and not the half order —but the large one. I was grateful. That was my all-time favorite fish dish and he was being generous. It was the most expensive item on the menu. He was not only respectful, but generous (thank you God). We then shared a decedent piece of chocolate cake which brought out the fun and lighthearted side of me.

We continued this way for a few months. It was slow and steady. This was new territory for me. He even suggested that we refrain from sex as we agreed it would change the dynamics of our new relationship that had begun to bloom into something completely foreign to me. We would remain pure. I once again had standards like I had as a young girl. Marc had qualities I yearned for. We both wanted to honor God, each other, our children and ourselves. He bought me a simple but personable neckless with a silver heart that had the number 33 on it. We both have a deep affection and fondness for this number because it has come to us in so many forms and signs. But mostly it represents Jesus and the years on earth he lived. I appreciated that we both shared the same attachment to this as well as so many other similarities. We had a lot of coincidences or as I like to call them "God incidences".

It was both a courtship and a meaningful friendship.

I had always met someone in the past and within days it became hot and heavy. This was different. It was warm, and light — imagine that…. I was dating. I was not rushing.

It wasn't romantic at first. We didn't flirt or get passionate until much later, this was a companionship that allowed me to learn about him. I saw him and could study him.

I saw him in a way I had seen no other.

I saw Jesus. I did. I saw his olive skin, his dark eyes and dark hair, his quiet and humble mannerisms, his soft touch with his hand in mine. I saw his devotion to me and now to the boys. I saw how he looked at me —not with lust or seduction, but with admiration and surrender. We talked for hours as though we were kids together. I thought of when I was little and although I had few friends, there was always one friend that I could go to, knock on the door and say, "Want to come out and play?"

That's how I felt around Marc. I just wanted to go out and play. I felt like I was at home with him. We took it slowly and within fifteen months, we would marry. I married my best friend. I married a man I feel safe with. We are so different.... It took time to adjust to us because our upbringings were so dissimilar. It is an ongoing process for me, and I know it is for most couples.

Although he couldn't relate to my childhood, neither did he punish me for it. He was supportive and grateful that I had come through so many hardships. Neither of us are perfect and we both fall short at times, but we try not to jump either. We all fall short. I just don't want to keep jumping over and over purposely, getting the same consequences and debilitating results. I learned the hard way it only causes more injury in my life.

We will have been married for three years this January. I love his parents. It's refreshing to have a solid and secure relationship with a second set of parents. He has two adult daughters and they are bright, intelligent and Godly ladies. I believe that because I let God direct this marriage and not me, we will be able to endure, where in past times I had failed. I've learned that we aren't competing. We are on the same team —each of us adding our own talents, gifts and abilities. In fact, I don't really enjoy competing as much as I have in the past. I like being part of a team and being right sized. — I'm not better than you and not less than you.

I'm just so happy that I get to run and that with all my injuries, the aging process and a horseback riding accident. The ride terrified me for the longest 10 minutes on her before she stopped abruptly and we both fell back. That occurred almost two years ago. I am still alive. I am not crippled. Because of that accident, I ended up with a fractured lumbar, a fractured sacral and a concussion. It was very debilitating for me and I wasn't quite the same afterwards.

My cognitive skills were affected. I couldn't remember what I was saying. I had a difficult time articulating what once had been second nature. I just wasn't as sharp as I had been before I fell off the horse. I was sensitive to lights and sounds. I had a hard time retaining anything I read or heard. It altered my work as a personal trainer. I needed to take time off to rest and to recover.

I had never taken a day off from school and rarely took a sick day at work unless it was to stay home with my sons when they were not feeling well. I needed to allow time to heal my brain and lower back. That is one of the reasons I decided to write this book. I had the time and I had the desire to write again. And I wanted to pursue my passion of writing. I had always journaled. As a little girl, I would write poetry that would start out as very raw, deep and despairing and end with hope, a way out and God as the finality. I also wrote letters to God. Today I believe that this is one of my purpose's, pursuits and quests, to continue putting pen to paper. So now I want to live out my purpose as well as live on purpose!

Because I was not able to absorb what I read and because I became easily confused and frustrated with myself, I was encouraged by my husband, friends and supervisor to seek out help for my concussion, so I did.

I sought out a CranioSacral massage therapist and she has been helpful. She treated me several times. She not only addressed my accident and helped me with the healing of my concussion, but she also helped me clear up some of my past issues where I had been "stuck."

So, as always, there was a silver lining to falling off a horse that had taken off with me on a ride from hell that ended when I fell off. It brought me to another healer and a second woman who is trained in EMDR and for this, I am eternally grateful. I'm not ashamed to get help for me today. I will ask for help over going backwards. I want to live today. Not die. I see too many lovely people suffer and die. I want to make it. Committing suicide is a permanent and irreversible act to a temporary setback and difficulty. I understand that dark, secluded and remote place. I have experienced and related to this a couple of times in my youth. But today I can ask for help. There is so much help. Asking for help is courageous. It is not weak. I remember a lady told me a few years ago that I was a woman of valor. I must confess I didn't know the meaning, so I looked it up and I teared up when I read its meaning. It takes fortitude and bravery to say I need support. I'm ok with that. I'm alive and I am present.

I have had so many beautiful people be "God with skin on" in my life. I have always had mothers and fathers along my path. Jenn has been like a mom to me. Bill has been like a dad. In fact, he walked me down the aisle when I got married a few years ago. My own mother is in a nursing home with people who have issues like hers. She is only seventy-one but cannot walk. She is wheelchair bound. I try and see her two to three times a year. She is up north, and it is difficult to get there more often. She is highly medicated, but most times she knows who I am. When I fly up to see her, she is giddy with happiness and elated to see me. We sing at the top of our lungs together —mostly old-time hymns, but we throw in some Elvis tunes too. She still laughs loudly and will cry just as quickly, and she is bound to her wheelchair now.

I believe she is at peace in her own world. I am happy for her that she can rest her mind, and most times I can accept her condition. I do wish she could jump out of that chair, hug me and nurture me and have a logical conversation about everything, truth be told about anything.

But she couldn't help being born with her illness. Still, it's not wrong for me wishing it was different. I've never envied others for having a coherent mom. I'm happy for them. I just wish sometimes I could call her and have a reasonable conversation, but it just wasn't in the cards. We get dealt the hand we get. I know it could be much worse and most times, I can truly believe it it's just those times when I gave birth, got married, miscarried my babies or needed a mom that I'd wish she could have been there. I don't fault her. I just miss her a lot. I miss my mom....

There were moments that she would smile fondly at me. She used to sneak the two of us out when my dad fell asleep. We would go out the window and walk a few blocks and sneak back in before he woke up. Believe it or not, those were very special moments. I miss the woman who went through hell and is now is in her own little heaven with pills pumping through her earthly body.

I love her. I wish I could help her. But the best thing I can do is call her, visit her and forgive her for not knowing how to do it any differently. For all of us, the greatest thing I can do right now is stay sane and break the chain, **And I have!**

Chapter 15

When I rehearse Gods victories in my life, I smile.

God's track record is perfect. If I can keep that in my mind, I fare much better.
My friend and mentor Mimi often say to me," Betty Jean. God will repay you for the years the Locusts have eaten." I love when I hear scripture spoken over me and she is right. Joel 2:25 will indeed take place in my life.

For many years I have felt like Job from the Old Testament. That man loved God through it all. He never lost his faith and loved God through all his trials and tribulations. I've never seen someone put through the fire as much as he was, and yet, he was blessed the later part of his life, more than his first. He was the real deal. Nothing is counterfeit about Job. He was vindicated in the end. I am declaring this over my life today as well as abundance and love.

My grandmother used to kiss her own hand as did my mom. Last night, as I was driving with Marc after a massage and dinner, I kissed *my* hand. It was precious. I nurture me today. The nourishment and deep need for attention is my responsibility. I can ask Marc for a hug. I can even spend time with my boys and friends, but deep down in my heart of hearts, I crave God. I create my own acceptance and fulfillment through him and our personal relationship. Only we can complete me and put me back together again.

All the resources and loving Angels along the way have assisted me. I am beyond grateful for every single spiritual and divine intervention. I've had agents of hope, thank God, my whole life, but at the end of the day when I get into bed next to my husband, I close my eyes and it's just God and me. I feel God's hands hold my face. I put my head to his chest, and I feel his heartbeat. I lean into his strong and loving arms and I say, "I love you Abba. I belong to you. Thank you for everything."

Most times I fall right to sleep, but not before I listen to my husband reading our devotions to me, including the Bible. He prays, and I sleep deeply. I am grateful for us. I include him on my gratitude list every day. I do an alphabet gratitude list. A is for acceptance. B is for the boys. Fast forward to M is for Marc. A grateful person won't slip into old ways. So, I stay grateful I feel that I have been transformed. I see a dramatic shift in me. I know it took long enough, but I have made that journey. I would never put up with what I put up with long ago. I also have learned to accept others as they are, not as I want them to be.

I've also accepted *me* for what and who I am and not what I *should* be.

God isn't surprised when I miss the mark. He likes me as I am. He celebrates me. I'm a big deal to Him. He sacrificed his life, so I could live. I am fifty-one— not that young, bombshell teenager I'd like to be at times. Menopause, life and age have altered me, and time has kicked my butt. I'm not a hundred years old, I've just realized that time is of the essence. I don't have time to waste! This is it. God still has work to do with me. I know that because I'm still breathing, I'm still here and I'm still alive! There has been a time and a season for every part of my life story. I believe that my ministry and purpose presently, is to write and to articulate to all of you, not just who I am, but *whose* I am. So, you too may receive that.

My heart says that I will have God's eyes and to be able to see *you* like only He can. Gods ears so that I will hear *you* like only He can. He will give *you* the hands to help you as needed, and the feet to walk where he does.

I know I can't save the world. I can only be a vessel. But if you do what I did and call out to Him and ask him into your heart and your life, —- you will never be alone. You will never be the same and you will never regret it. I haven't.

Now that I have written this book, I am so pleased. It is one less regret I will have. I am doing what I have thought about for years. I want to inspire and encourage you to do the same. I vacillated and floundered about putting it all out there, but it was time. Is it your time too? I know I will celebrate you either way. I will rally around you. I want you to achieve every goal, overcome every dilemma and every set back. I want all of us to make it. I believe it is our providence.

Thank you for celebrating mine. Although I don't regret anything now that happened with my dad, I do wish he could be here with me. I was able to be with him in his last days.   He had a diabetic stroke when he was only fifty-eight years old.   After the stroke, his body deteriorated and his will to live was weakened. I personally believe he was too tired to continue. I wish I could see him now in order to tell him that I love him and want to talk to him. Before he died, Hospice cared for him for a week. They were so compassionate, tender and kind. I got to spend a lot of time with him ......We didn't say much, but I showed up every day between clients, even if it was only for fifteen minutes. I just wanted to see his face.

He was so frail and thin. Not the strong, tall and intimidating man I would cower from as a child.   He was a ghost of his former self. He looked twice his age— if that was possible. My father never told me he was sorry for anything when he was alive. Many years later, I had a vision of him.   One where he was standing at a fence. He came to me and said,

'Betty Jean. I am sorry for what you have experienced. If I knew it would have affected you so much, I would have never done those things to you, please forgive me. I need you to do that, please. I can't go on either if you don't forgive me.'

I sobbed. I was blown away. I told him that I forgave him. I thanked him and he thanked me. He told me that time is short, and to enjoy my life. Then he turned around and walked away.
I tell you I felt such a release— a freedom. By completely forgiving him and moving on, he also was "unstuck" and loosed.

I think about an inmate who is freed from his jail term. He walks out of the building in his orange jumpsuit and he can change into his own clothes. Instead, he chooses to walk around outside of jail wearing his old prison jumpsuit. How on earth will he ever work, enjoy family and friends walking around as though he was still in jail? He has been set free!

I needed to start living it! That was me for years. I have been set free from my prison so many times and still I chose to walk around like I was incarcerated and confined.

I's OK. I'm out of that now. I just need to remember not to put on those handcuffs, chains and that jumpsuit again.

I am free. Free indeed. I have been released and it's up to me to not come back.
I am not even getting close to those threads. I've walked far, far away from that old lock up facility and I haven't looked back except for one last goodbye— for the last time!

I have explored my ancestry in the last 6 months. I knew growing up that we were of German descent and it was confirmed by research. It was fun and an all-consuming figuring out my heritage. It led me to go back to Philly a couple of months ago with my sister, Barbie who flew up with me. We saw my siblings, cousins and family. It was a special reunion for all of us.

On our way back, before we went to the airport, Barbie and I had a few hours and decided to visit all the places that we grew up in —including our Grandparents' places. I didn't go back to reminisce or to relive it all over again.   In fact, I was neutral. I just wanted to not forget either. I went not really expecting anything.

We went to the first house in Ridley Park.   I couldn't believe how tiny the home was, but even more surprising to me was how close the railroad tracks were to the small house, —-only about five hundred feet away. The backyard no longer backed up to the Woods. Instead, new homes had been built in its place. I had to see it as an adult.   It had been forty-six years since I ran out of those Woods to safety. I am so darn grateful for my sister, Barbie, who was by my side as we drove slowly next to where the Woods were back in 1971. It was surreal for me. I could still see the train tracks.

 As we stopped at the stop sign to make a right, we slowly turned, and God as my witness, a man about forty years old, with a long beard and suspenders was walking on the sidewalk right where the Woods were. I gasped and said, "Oh God!"

 The man was staring at us. I couldn't believe my eyes. We passed him slowly and I belted out a scream. Barbie asked if I wanted to pull over, but I continued to drive. I am OK. Oh my gosh!
I can't believe it, but that looks exactly like the man who molested me!

Of course, it wasn't that man from 1971 because he would be about 85 by now. But it was a vision I will never forget.

I am so relieved that I had another pair of eyes to witness this with me. I had just, for the second time, divulged to her what happened to me at age five— just minutes before we saw him. There are so many ways to look at this and, quite honestly, I could analyze it until the cows come home. But what seems to resonate the most for me is, **I got away. I survived,** and he can't get me. He didn't then and he won't now. I escaped... and I broke free. I need to celebrate that and not live in the past any longer wondering why it happened. Why any of the traumatic things have happened. They did happen. I survived. I remember the first time I read the poem "Footprints in the Sand" at about age 15. I was incensed when I got to the part that said: "But I have noticed that during the most troublesome times in my life there is only one set of footprints. I don't understand why when I needed you the most you would leave me." I can see me folding my arms across my chest and being a bit sassy with God for a split second "Yeah God, where were you anyway?" Before continuing to read," The Lord replied: "My precious child, I love you and would never leave you. During your times of trial and suffering, when you see only one set of footprints, it was then that I carried you.' I sobbed like I am right now. He was there with me in

161

every single moment and he never left me. He never forsook me. I don't blame God. I don't blame me.

I can't thank my mom enough for introducing me to my faith, and my father for teaching me to be strong, street smart and clever. Without my brokenness, how could the light shine through? Every challenge has matured me and given me an opportunity to grow, love, heal and respond positively rather than react negatively. I so appreciate that my sister, who has been through it all with me, was here again beside me. I love my siblings so much. We have a special bond that has kept us moving forward. They have been my constant. As we drove to the next house that we had shared, I thanked God for the fact that I hadn't needed to look in the rearview mirror at the man who looked like that same train conductor from long ago. I didn't need to turn the car around to take a picture or the need to see him again. I kept driving and looking straight ahead —out the windshield in front of me. It had never looked so good and so clear.

When I returned home, I shared what had happened with my husband. He is such a great listener. He was so pleased for my healing process. I also explained how most of my father's side came from Bucks County and way back, from the Lower Alsace, and Reichweiler, Germany. I started to research the area and where I would like to go, and Marc is willing to send me. I would like to go with my boys or friends as Marc would rather do a trip to another country. I am grateful we can trust each other to go places on our own. There was a time I may have been insecure about being without him and although I love him as my traveling mate as well as my husband it is healthy for our relationship to do things apart at times. But we are both going to Israel.

I have been dreaming about going to Israel for about twenty years and I know Marc and I will make this journey at some point.   We want to be baptized again, but this time in the Jordan River. I can't wait until we go. We still have the responsibility of my youngest son at home so for now, it's a bucket list item until he goes off to college. I have now been able to visit forty-one states in the USA. I especially enjoyed Laguna Beach California, Vail Colorado, NYC, Chicago Illinois, Seattle Washington and Kennebunkport, Maine. Next month I am planning on visiting Wisconsin, Iowa, Nebraska and South Dakota with my son Tyler. I am excited about this. I have loved traveling, but I must admit I have decided to no longer travel *back* in time anymore after fifty-one years. I have traveled backwards more than enough. It has been necessary for me get to where I am right now.   I have needed every single moment, but it's time now to move forward.

163

I have so much more left to do. I can continue helping people in any way possible. Everyday there is an opportunity right in front of me. With my husband, my sons, my family members, — with each client I train or with the cashier at the store. I have learned not to flaunt what I do for others, but to keep it between me and God and I like that....That has been one of my favorite highs ever —to do something kind without getting found out, whether it's a monetary deed, like seeing someone in need and taking care of it, or helping a homeless person; perhaps even just a smile, hug or kind word to someone who is dying to be loved.

I mentor woman and just try to be mindful wherever I go. I am not perfect. I fall short daily, but I keep on trying. Today I can walk up to anyone at any time and extend my hand and smile. I belong everywhere now!

I don't need to look down at my feet today. I can look you in the eye and I can even look myself in the eye. I like what I see, in spite of the wrinkles, the gray hair and the little imperfections. I see past the obvious and look down deep into my heart and soul and I see who God sees now. I see a strong, capable, loving woman and I hear God whisper the most gorgeous words that I pray to hear when I meet him face to face,

"Well done my good and faithful servant, my beloved daughter, I love you. Be loved!"

Epilogue

Writing this has been both healing and emotional. There is a part of me that does not want to expose me or expose the people in my life. I want everyone to be looked at in a good light, — including me. This is a delicate matter. I also believe that it Is not all about me.

If I can help someone by communicating my story and by sharing my testimony about how God can help you overcome whatever the issues are, it will have been worth it. I can't do God justice, but He surely has done His justice in me. I believe God downloaded my story in my heart to share with you.

In no way am I "free sailing" now. I must continue to be vigilant and stay with the basics, so that I never have to go back to them. It is hard work for me. I need to make sure I get enough sleep and rest. I need to continue to eat healthy and exercise 3-5x a week. I need my support group and my girlfriends who hold me accountable. Laurie, Mimi, Elizabeth, Jenn, Letty, Shortcake and my sister Barbie are my confidants and my constant companions. I know I could trust them with my kids and my credit card! I am blessed to have that assurance and sisterhood. They have been with me for most of my life.   I know when I am struggling or feeling down that I need help and I need to ask for help and not be ashamed to seek out a counselor. It has continued to work for me. If I get too busy for God and for me, I am too busy!

I also love my quiet time up on the mountain —like Jesus did. He went up to pray and spend time with God and if it was good enough for Him it only makes sense to follow suit. Sometimes, all I need is a few minutes. There are other times when I may need to go on a retreat or to just be still and enjoy my one on one time with God. God loves my "kneel mail." God loves when I turn up the volume on the music and worship, sing and dance for him.

I think at times I feel like I need to figure out everything. I have a hard time waiting in the hallway when it's my nature to kick down doors. I am learning that I can pause and trust God and know that he is working on my behalf. I can breathe and let go and let God be God. He knows tomorrow's headlines. He sees around corners. Nothing surprises God. Nothing broadsides Him.

I remember when my boys were babies, I would put them in the car seat in the back. As infants, they never asked me where we were going. They trusted that wherever we drove, I would take care of them. They looked out the window and off we went. I want that kind of trust and assurance with God. I want to get strapped in and say, 'Ok *Daddy. Let's go. Wherever you take me I can enjoy the ride!'*

I don't always know where I am being led, but I do know that I'm not lost. I am being guided by my capable and all-knowing Father. I don't need to be led by my emotions, feelings or attitudes. I can bypass all that now and trust in His word that never changes. I don't need to try and convince God of anything. I may try. But in the end, He ends up needing to convince me. His ways are always better than mine. He does know it all. He does know how many hairs I have on my head. He calls me by name. My fingerprint is like no other. When things don't work out like I think they should, I must remember that I don't know everything. I don't know the whole plot — only my Father does. He will work everything out for my good because I love him, and He loves me. I read the Good Book. It says that we will win in the end. It doesn't mean it won't be difficult. Thankfully the bible never needs to be revised. What is in it is true and unchanging.

When I lift weights, I need to use effort and strength. I count the repetitions and I need to push through. I also know when it's time to rest and to allow my body to recover. It's a constant balancing act. I take it one step at a time. I know it's not a competition against others or against me. I am for me. God is for me. If God is for me who can be against me? Not even me. Those days are gone. I am: *Pro love - Pro God - Pro family - Pro unity - Pro kindness - Pro others - Pro me.* Even when it is a struggle, I lift my head and stay where my feet are. I breathe. I pause. I continue. I make the effort God takes care of the outcome.

The bottom line and reality? Life can be difficult. It certainly was for Jesus. I don't know of one tragedy that he escaped. He was rejected, doubted, falsely accused, denied, hated, misunderstood, betrayed, ridiculed, tempted, abandoned and ultimately tortured and killed. Why would I believe my life would be a "bowl of cherries?" I can go to my savior and he understands every one of my heartaches. And in the end, He was risen. I have risen in a sense too — out of the ashes.

I've also learned that God supplies the bait, but I must do the fishing. We have a relationship that takes two. Sometimes he requires more of me than from others. He says, *'Lean into me and let me carry you.'* It's in knowing His voice. I can't hear Him if I'm all over the place.

I can remember my 'Mom Mom's ' voice at age nine. I would recall it now if I heard it again. I know my father's voice. Sometimes I hear it in another person, — a mentor, a child, in nature. Sometimes I hear it inside of me and in His beautiful abundance of letters called the Bible. His love letters speak to me and are a light to direct my path. The word of God is true. But make no mistake, there is a dark force that wants to rob me of my joy. That force wants to break through, and I must gird myself with the full armor of God. Not a "hand-me" down armor, but the real deal. I must wear the belt of truth, righteousness, faith, a helmet of salvation and the sword of the spirit. I must be alert and in prayer because I am weak. The great news is, my Abba is stronger. His victory is irrevocable and inevitable.

This requires audacious faith from me, but I do know it works—when I work it. I've seen it with my own eyes repeatedly, both with others and with me.

I wish I could radiate joy every moment, but that just isn't possible. I do smile often. It makes me happy to smile and to see others smile back. But even if they can't, I still smile often. Certainly, more than when I was growing up. I don't burn myself out anymore with performances or success. I already have. I'm enough. I can start my day over if I start out on the wrong foot. It doesn't need to consume me and take days.

Most days, I need to pause and make sure I'm not too hungry, angry, lonely or tired.

Look, nothing I've done is going to get me on the 11 pm news. I am more like you than either of us may realize. I want to make new friends. I'm not afraid. I want to visit new places and experience new things and not rush through just to arrive at the next event.

I've learned to run my races with a smile and to cheer on my fellow runners who go whizzing by me. I might even see a flower and stop to pick it up or talk to a fellow runner as we run side by side. I'm in the moment these days. I will take that over a faster pace where I must mentally go somewhere else. I'm grateful

169

for those wins. If need be, I can use my mind over matter like my Grandmother used to tell me. If I just want to run for the health of it, that's good enough for me too. I will continue to write about my trips and family and friends. I will also continue to speak to others who have gone through similar situations knowing we can overcome and be triumphant. We can come up from the ashes into His marvelous light.

Now that the worst is behind me, I want to make new memories. I still see the scar above my lip. It may be there forever. But it doesn't hurt anymore. It happened. It's visible at times, but it's not the first thing you see on me today. It doesn't define me. My past has affected me. That is a truth I've learned *in spite of* the trauma, I am not a casualty. I am a darn miracle!

Amen! 33   (That is my number, the number of years JESUS walked on this earth.)

Made in the USA
Coppell, TX
02 August 2020